Marked For Life, Not Scarred!

Cynthia Demola-Oliveira

ISBN 978-1-64349-330-5 (paperback)
ISBN 978-1-64349-331-2 (digital)

Christian Faith Publishing, Inc.
832 Park Avenue
Meadville, PA 16335
www.christianfaithpublishing.com

Printed in the United States of America

To my *father*, David T. Demola, the *most* amazing human being I will ever meet. Your faith and love—the essence of who God is has preserved me. I am everything I am because of you and your faith in our Savior, Who He is and who I am in Him. I honor you with this book with the conviction you have which has taught me (and is still teaching me) to love people and to reach out and to believe that it will help set people free from their past and will drive them into their destiny. It is all about that *grace*.

To my *husband*, PJ, the next best David T. Demola, for sure. You are strength when I am weak. You speak when I cannot. You carry me when I cannot walk. My life really did begin when I met you. I love you more than I could ever say. It is amazing to ride this wave with you, and we are on its crest, surfing to our true calling…

"I have the mark of the promise.
I have the mark of the
promise that HE made.
Who could ever erase that seal on me?
What could ever block it if I have
already decided who I am?
My God NEVER fails!
I know my time has come.
He has changed my luck, right
before my very eyes."

Prologue

Every year, 3.3 million reports of child abuse are made in the United States involving nearly 6 million children (a report can include multiple children). The United States has the worst record in the industrialized nations—losing five children every day due to abuse-related deaths.

The real prevalence of child sexual abuse is not known because so many victims do not disclose the awful experiences they had. I was one of them. For many years, I refused to admit I was molested, convincing myself that the attention I received was love. People react very differently to sexual molestation and abuse. Some people become angry and hate the perpetrator or seek vengeance. Others shut down completely and struggle emotionally their whole lives. Many continue to engage in the same dreadful behavior that was inflicted upon them, and the vicious cycle continues. The implications of what was done to me as a little girl, and even later as a teenager and young adult, were not realized until much later in my life.

Every inappropriate word, gesture, touch to a child has the potential to rob them of their young and innocent life and will even affect their very purpose in life—their destiny—if not dealt with. This consuming and wicked process has the potential to overshadow and continue to torment its victims throughout the course of their life. I experienced firsthand the pervasive theme of shame and a nagging guilty conscience without truly understanding the origin. I covered these feelings with emotional eating and rebellion to rules. It was all an attempt to rob me of my destiny and destroy my life. My destiny is as yet not fully known, but at the very least; I know that I was placed on earth to support my father and his ministry, to love my husband and son, to teach, to bring healing, and to encourage. I wrote this book to share my very personal thoughts and experiences from some of the deep dark places of my life. I wrote to help rescue people from the prison cells of their minds, even if they are of our own making.

It is possible to be free of our past and to be inundated with the light of God's goodness into completeness. Your life is valuable! Healing is available and possible. I hope my process and this book will help you realize your path out of pain and into victory. For me, this process has become a very big step in discovering and living my own destiny. At one time, I would have been embarrassed to share such personal mistakes and pain and the secret suffering that ensued, but I realize the power of the pen. A very wise man of God (and very good friend—Robert) told me that when God wanted to communicate, He wrote a book. I know you will feel this power too if you will open your heart and put away your shame and your preconceived notions. Healing comes in many forms and is always available when received. It is *never* too late to pursue your dream and to release the pain and shame of the hurts and sins of the past. Grace is new every single day. Cash in on it, and do not ever look back with shame again.

Love and faith and grace.

"He has made everything beautiful
and appropriate in its time.
He has also planted eternity
(a sense of DIVINE PURPOSE)
in the human heart
(a mysterious longing which
nothing under the sun can satisfy,
except GOD)—yet man cannot
find out what God has done
(His overall plan) from the
beginning to end."

~Ecclesiastes 3:11~

Chapter 1

Trust Your Gut

For some reason, I have this terrible tendency to question and requestion, think and rethink, and do and redo everything. Well, not really everything, only the things I do that may come across harsh or negative or things that may appear selfish or are grossly misinterpreted by others. I even question my own creative ideas, yet I accept other people's creative expressions as is. My own actions and thoughts are constantly on trial in my own mind, usually with a hung jury.

I am doing my best to stop whatever it is that causes me to do this. I need to learn to trust my gut more. I need to be confident not only in what I can do and say, but in who I am. Most of us need to believe that when we dream or speak or act, it is coming from the right place, from the deepest part of us. I am learning that I need to trust that my personal life lessons, and the years of education are the very essence of who I am becoming, and have been orchestrated by the gracious Creator of life. I can trust me. I can easily discern right and wrong. I can choose better over good, and I can know best over better. I can trust my gut, the heart of me, resting in the fact that it will all be okay. Trust means following. Following requires action. It is trust that prepares me, but it is action that puts me in the ring and positions me for the win.

*****

I was standing in front of the kitchen sink in my parent's house. My niece, Giavanna, walked behind. It was her birthday, and the family was together to celebrate. She was nine and so excited to be turning ten; the picture-perfect little girl complete with porcelain skin, long shiny black ponytails that curled just enough, and one dimple on her left cheek to highlight her adorable smile. She loved all the things most little girls do at that age: hopscotch, gummy bears, macaroni and cheese, stuffed animals, and every other fun thing you can think of. Her mother, my sister Jodi, often commented about how Giavanna reminded her of me. She was smart and quick-witted but slow to engage. She loved to talk to her dolls and animals, and her long dark curls contrasted her ivory skin, like mine. I could see the excitement on Giavanna's face as she was looking up at me. She could hardly stand the wait, anxious to devour the cake of her choice and then rip open her gifts while we all sang "Happy Birthday." First, we would feast on the usual Italian dinner favorites: delicious hand-crafted ravioli; chicken meatballs full of fresh parsley, garlic, and imported grated Romano cheese; sweet and spicy hot sausages; beef braciole; sautéed broccoli or broccoli rabe; and a huge salad tossed with crisp fresh greens, nuts, and olives delicately balanced with balsamic vinegar and first-pressed, extra virgin olive oil. A few loaves of fresh bakery semolina bread rounded out the perfect meal.

Giavanna asked for soda. I leaned down to pour some icy cold Sprite into a red oversized plastic cup. As I watched her small hand struggle to wrap around that big cup, my mind began to wander back to my tiny hands. Suddenly, I felt a little warm, and I became aware of my own heartbeat. I felt my breathing become more rapid, and I felt light-headed and in need of some fresh air. I was ten once too. The age of coloring books, Magic Markers, and do-it-yourself crafts with all those annoying beads that always bounce all over the place. I wanted every Barbie ever made and every Barbie accessory I could find. If I could not find what I wanted, or if we could not afford what I found, I tried to make it, and this was often the case. When it was time to play outside, I was just as enthusiastic about freeze tag and Red Rover as I was about riding my bicycle or coloring the sidewalk with hearts and flowers and hopscotch boards. We would write our names and initials and whatever else we could think of. We used thick colored chalks that barely fit in my hands. They made my hands uncomfortably dry and my clothes chalky white. At night, I played with plastic ovens and kitchen utensils, pretending to cook plastic foods serving them to my dolls.

Ten is the age when you know enough to learn and share and be yourself without fear of what others think. You speak your mind. You are young enough to enjoy all the pleasures you have been newly experiencing in life. You ask for what you want and expect to get it. It is the age of ponytails, headbands, and birthstone earrings. Ten is the age where school is still kind of fun and boys are kind of cool, but not cool enough to be your friends. You can still pretend to be a princess, and although fashion matters a little bit, it does not matter enough to interfere with life. Ten is innocent. Ten is an age full of hope and dreams. Ten is so very young and precious.

Somewhat awakened from my momentary stupor but still sort of frozen in my thoughts, I continued to stand there long after my niece walked away. I could not believe that anyone could see a ten-year-old child in a sexual way. Sick, that is what it was. Sick and demented and demonic.

On that day, I realized just how tragic it was to have my childhood innocence taken from me as easily as a toll collector takes the fare from a driver on the New Jersey Turnpike. Sweating with a rapid heartbeat and the slight feeling of faint, for the first time ever, I was really mad at *him*. Seeing my beautiful niece forced me to think back to a time in my life that was previously well hidden in the dark closet of my own making. I had kept it in the dark for far too long, and now it was exposed. The light was on, never to be turned off again.

Chapter 2

Fear: *Feed your faith and your fear will starve to death.*

At least four times a week I drive by Newark Liberty International Airport. Lately, especially if my sweet stepson, Jordon is in the car, we love to watch the planes take off and count the ones lined up in the sky waiting to land. I get genuinely excited (and loud about it, Jordon would say) if a plane is landing and is parallel to our position on the road.

I had been enjoying these moments for quite a while, but one day, the joy of the moment brought me back to another time of my life when I purposely avoided driving anywhere near the airport. This may appear both insignificant and easy to do, but when you live and work in the New York, New Jersey Metropolitan area, it is not so easily avoided. There are three international airports within about thirty miles of each other. I had been flying since I was a young girl and was very familiar and used to it. But somehow over the years, I managed to let fear grow big, overtake me, and eventually stop me. For years I became so tense about flying and especially landing that I stopped flying completely. I remember the fear I felt, complete with my heart racing, hands trembling, and beads of sweat barely staying above my brow. I even experienced a dry mouth and tense neck at the slightest bump during the flight, which eventually became the last straw to break the proverbial camel's back. That "OH MY GOD" sick stirring in my stomach prompted me to think positive thoughts and recite affirmations of faith especially when I heard and felt the landing gear. The memory of those feelings (not the other hundreds of perfect hours in flight and textbook landings) overtook me, and I could no longer bring myself to get on a plane. That meant I stopped vacations, visiting friends, ministry trips, you name it. I even won a trip to California early in my college education. It would have been an amazing trip with expenses paid to Napa Valley, complete with vineyard tours, wine tastings, and perfect weather. But I was too afraid to fly, so I never went.

If I did have to drive near an airport, I would sweat and pant and shake (full-fledged anxiety in motion). I would hit the gas so fast to get it over with for fear a plane would crash or explode, or worse— land on my car. Now, when is the last time you heard of something like this happening? Yet for too many years, I made this ridiculous fear my reality. It stopped me in my tracks. Sometimes, feeling full-fledged panic, I would have to pull over to get myself together. I let the tiny seed of fear that came in the form of a very unrealistic thought get planted and take root, and I would not drive anywhere near an airport, never mind get on a plane.

If we are focused on negative things, if we magnify a passing thought that we should have filtered out immediately, this thought will begin to take root and grow with the potential to cause sense-less worry and a lot of pain. Conversely, if we magnify the tiniest thoughts of success and hope—feeding them with imagining and believing and seeing them as coming true—they will grow. We can water these seeds of faith with positive words and positive actions. We cannot control the weather. We cannot control the amount of sun and rain and the storms that come, but we can do our best to preserve the seed faith by speaking and believing all that is good, contrasting the negative with positive. We can use the storm to preserve and prepare the seed.

Starving our doubts strips them of any power because they cannot thrive. To handle these unreal and unruly fears that were dictating how I should live, I made a decision to confront them. It took a little bit of time and certain steps, like realizing I was not fully engaged in living my life and knowing I had to take authority over my racing thoughts. I got a job working in Newark, New Jersey, where I had to drive by the airport daily. This helped me confront my fear head-on and was my way of telling my fear to shut up as I gripped the steering wheel, stepping heavily on the gas.

After a few years of that constant confrontation, I felt strong enough to fly. I booked a trip to Mexico—flying alone. I was meeting friends there, but I traveled all by myself. I sat back in my seat thinking that the worst thing that could happen is I crash and I die, and once I realized that I did not have control over the worst, I could speak to myself and my situation and enjoy the flight. So I did. I ordered a Coca-Cola with a lot of ice (my favorite comfort item on a plane), sat back, breathed deeply, and was calm enough to actually enjoy the flight. Once you are "locked and loaded" on a plane, you have no way out. For sanity (and the sanity of the people near you), you have no choice but to quiet your mind down. I had no control over that plane, but I did have control over my mind and my thoughts and where I placed my trust. I told myself and the plane that we were going to land safely. When I felt fear, I chose to ignore it and to feed my faith, saying, "This will be a great, safe flight, and I have a lot more living to do," and my doubts began to starve and subside on that very flight.

I enjoyed the beautiful Caribbean after having missed it for so long. Tanning and swimming and dining with my friends were even better after having conquered my fear of flying again. The sand was brighter, the sun was warmer, and everything was just a little bit sweeter. I flew back home happy and safe, putting to sleep that fear and burying it once and for all. I now fly anywhere and anytime I want to. My most recent flight was a ten-hour, international flight, and it was amazing.

I consciously make daily choices to think faith-filled thoughts over fear-filled thoughts. This sets the pace for success, regardless of what obstacle I have, and I have many obstacles. Let's face it, we all do. Do we hurdle over them or do they stop us dead in our tracks? Circumstances will not stop us unless we permit them to. Although they may often appear to be stopping us and although they even delay us, obstacles cannot stop us from our destiny. Only we can stop us. The course for our path of success is set. We have to walk the path, avoiding impasses and hurdling obstacles no matter how much it hurts to jump them. Sometimes we may lengthen the path or obscure it or even make the path a bit narrower and more treacherous; but no matter what we have done, our destiny is not only within reach it is inevitable.

Chapter 3

Moving

I do not really remember a whole lot of my childhood at home. I am sure this is a choice. I mean, I remember a lot of details from elementary school and middle school, and I could recount to you every teacher and much of what I learned in each grade. I was always in the "advanced placement" or AP classes with a bunch of smart kids who came from upper-class families, though we were lower middle class. I liked school, I still do. I loved learning, and being with really smart kids kept me on my toes. I can name most of those kids to this day and a few of their names you might even recognize. They were special people and probably still are. I remember competitive spelling bees and storytelling contests. I was naturally good at language and arts, and I loved that our AP class started learning French in fifth grade. As I continued through middle school, I felt proud to be in the National Honor Society and the National French Honor Society and to participate in some of the scholastic clubs, like the debate club and the chess club. Although I could hold my own at chess I was not really a good player, but I was comfortable with those kids, and it was fun to learn from them.

I feel as though my home memories are not quite as detailed. When I was really young, our whole family lived with Grandma and Grandpa, and I loved it. Though my paternal grandparents were first-generation Americans, they lived like Italian immigrants. Most people live what they know, learning a lot about life from their parents, especially back in those days. I loved having Grandpa and Daddy in the same house. It was pure joy. I felt safe. Every night in our bunk beds, my sister Jodi, who slept in the top bunk, would figure out a way to scare me and challenge the secure feeling I had. I would get up, tiptoe to the next room, and tap my grandma on the shoulder to wake her up. Without words, she would roll over to the edge of her bed and let me jump over her and slip into the middle of the bed, between her and my grandfather. I was safe, warm, and comfortable between Grandma and Grandpa, without a care in the world. I slept comfy and sound.

Being in an Italian American family was special. I guess this is true of all families. We are taught that our culture is the best and that we should feel proud. We were lower middle class, and my grandfather and father worked hard to be that. Joseph Demola—Grandpa—was born to a single mother in Brooklyn, New York, who married soon thereafter. His new stepfather introduced stepsiblings to my grandfather, and he loved them very much throughout his lifetime. Grandpa was such a hard worker, holding many interesting jobs through his life including being a lifeguard at the public beaches in Brooklyn and Staten Island as a teenager and a NYC firefighter, where he eventually became fire chief. In his spare time, he was either training or sparring for the Golden Gloves boxing title in Jersey City or playing with all his might on another team sport. He was a tough New York City guy, raised in Bensonhurst, Brooklyn; and although he sounded like a tough New Yorker, he had a heart of gold. He and his brother-in-law, my Uncle Frank, opened and co-owned a small hardware store on Staten Island, at about the time he entered into full-time ministry. In those days, most preachers in smaller churches supplemented their income with some sort of side work—they had to—just to feed their families. The hardware store was close and convenient to both of their homes and did pretty well, serving the local community. As time went on, the neighborhood began to change. Families were moving out of the neighborhood, and strangers were moving in, making the store less of a neighborhood friendly place and more vulnerable to whatever may be. One early evening, a young man walked in, placed a revolver to Grandpa's temple, and demanded all the cash that was in the register. He handed over the money and left there without a physical scratch, surely protected from what could have been a horrible tragedy: He and my Uncle Frank used that week to discuss permanently closing the store. After the entire family heard and recounted that awful event, the decision was to continue business as usual, although my grandfather was the only one who had to push through. He was the one whose life was threatened. He was the one who was traumatized. One week after re-opening, that same young guy came back and put that same gun to my grandfather's head as he again forced my grandfather to hand over all the money from the register. Protected again, my grandfather left the store and never went back. They shut it down forever and moved into the next part of their lives. My grandfather was a kind, honest man who taught us many life lessons. He was my first pastor, and running the hardware store was the only other job he held that I personally witnessed. I spent a lot of hours with him watching him live a genuine life of helping people in any way he could.

My grandmother was a very simple woman. Her name was Angelina Rose, but everyone called her "Sister Rose" because she had always hated the name Angelina. She grew up an only child on a farm in Pennsylvania with just her mother who (I am told) did not like her daughter very much. Grandma Rose met and married Joseph Demola at the tender age of sixteen. They lived in Staten Island with Grandma's mother (Grandma Nanootz to my dad and his brothers.) I never met great-Grandma Nanootz because she died before I could know her, but that is probably a good thing because stories of her always sound a little intimidating. Grandma Rose worked as a seamstress in a factory. She made us many of our church dresses and summer outfits. She loved to laugh, and her passion was shopping, but family was everything to her. We were all very close to my paternal grandparents. They were amazing people with warm hearts and generous hands, and they passed those traits down to my father, for sure. Their lives were about God, family, and people. Who wouldn't want to be with them as much as possible? My grandparents did not speak much Italian at home, though hearing the language of my ancestors spoken between them and at church for the Italian service always felt special. I did not hear it enough to learn it, and like most second- and third-generation Americans, I had no motivation to learn it anyway.

Sundays were all about the Italian Pentecostal church my grandpa helped start. Church services were held in English Sunday mornings and Sunday nights, and for most of us who attended that church, there was the traditional early Sunday dinner in the middle of the day after morning service. Sunday dinner featured some sort of pasta, like spaghetti, linguini, or ziti along with garlicky meatballs, sausage, and other cuts of beef and pork simmered slowly in tomato sauce that was usually made the day before. Salad and fresh Italian bread were a necessary accompaniment, and the salad always was eaten at the end of the meal to "help digest." Many times, this meal was shared with our extended family, and for my family, that meant going to Uncle Joe's house. Uncle Joe (Joseph Demola II) was the middle brother (my dad's older brother) whom he was closest to. He was a contractor in the city, and he played the organ at church. He was really funny and a fun-loving guy, who always had a big smile on his face, a joke on his tongue, and a heavy-handed pat on the back for someone in need. If the family was all together for Sunday dinner at Uncle Joe's, we got to feast on other typical but fancier Italian specialties like antipasto with imported provolone, prosciutto, and salami. Since the cured meats were not enough, next to them was usually a tray of fresh, salted mozzarella atop sweet garden-grown tomatoes kissed with fruity imported virgin olive oil and a healthy sprinkle of salt. Aunt Vera would always have some sort of meat like a deliciously seasoned roast beef or a stuffed roast pork or baked chicken pieces bathed in lemon and fresh herbs cooking in the oven and filling the house with a heavenly aroma. Accompanying the meat was skillfully sautéed broccoli rabe or escarole with white beans, crushed red pepper flakes, and whole cloves of barely golden sautéed garlic. Manicotti, ravioli, and lasagna were usually reserved for holidays, and there were always fresh fruits and authentic bakery-bought Italian pastries for dessert. Many Sunday nights after church, especially if we did not eat together in the afternoon, we went to Uncle Joe's house for homemade pizza and fried calzones that he and Dad made together. Uncle Joe used to always trick me into eating a hot pepper, swearing it wasn't hot and laughing until he coughed while I suffered through the pain after swallowing it. I would desperately seek ice water to cool my burned tongue while everyone laughed at my naivety. Being together was the best, but none of this abundance of delicious, high-calorie food was good for my already-height-challenged physique with a tendency to grow horizontally faster than vertically. I never worried about it while we were together, but it would become a central issue in my life. I loved being with my older cousins. The laughing, fellowship, and eating—especially if Daddy, Grandpa and Uncle Joe were making pizza and fried dough—were priceless.

We lived with my grandparents on Staten Island (the forgotten borough of NYC), in the humble birth home of my father, until I was ready to start kindergarten. Grandma always liked to tell us how Daddy had to be born at home because there was an outbreak of measles in Staten Island, and it was safer for them both to stay home rather than go to the hospital. That made the house even more special. I was always a Daddy's and Grandpa's girl, so I spent hours being with either one or both of them, doing whatever it was they were doing. I used to sit on my grandfather's lap for hours drawing in his Bible while he studied at the dining room table that was always covered in protective plastic. If I got tired of sitting on his lap, I would sit on a dining room chair, and my legs would stick to the plastic, but I didn't care. I wanted to be close to him. If I wasn't sitting with Grandpa there, I was following him in the yard while he tended to his pear trees, fig trees, or tomato plants. If I wasn't with Grandpa doing something, I was with my dad at the church or on a carpentry job. After school, I would come home and immediately go unlock and open the tiny metal gate behind our house. The gate led to a short rocky path through a small lot of woods, which led to a large asphalted driveway that was directly behind our house. My grandfather created that rocky path between our house and my friend Dianne's house for easy passage. I would spend most of the afternoon there playing. Dianne had all the newest toys, a big yard complete with a huge oak tree, with a super thick limb that grew parallel to the ground and was perfect for hanging out on. We would climb up and sit in that tree for hours, safe from the real world and lost in our imaginary one. Behind the L-shaped driveway at Dianne's house was a detached, two story building which contained six garages on the first floor and storage space on the second, all of which could be rented. We believed the second story space was additional play space, just for us. There, our fantasies came to life. It was a class-room, a church, a space station, even a nursery or zoo, depending on whether we had dolls or stuffed animals. If that storage space, her bedroom, her grandparents' third-floor apartment that was gener-ously made available to us weren't enough, Dianne also had a huge basement we were also allowed to play in stocked with everything her grandparents could buy her. She was so different than me in so many ways, but we were two peas in a pod for playtime, and we always had a lot of conversation and a lot of laughs. Although we were so young, our cultural differences were obvious. She was so American—blonde and blue eyed, tall and thin. Dianne lived with her single, divorced mother who was a nurse and cooked and ate things like fish cakes and casseroles and baked salmon aside seasoned rice from a box. Her grandparents were neighbors of my grandparents for many years, and they lived on the third floor of a three-floor house that they owned for about as long as my grandparents owned theirs. I could never understand why her grandfather always had a semichewed, unlit cigar in his mouth. It was foreign to me, a traditionally raised church girl who barely had a clue what a cigar was. Dianne and her mother and their giant, shaggy dog Honey lived on the second floor of their house. The concept of a single mother was foreign to me. I did not understand why she had no father. My young mind did not relate to or understand divorce and the concept of parenting from afar. But life as I knew it was good, which is why I did not understand the idea of moving when I first heard my parents talk about it. My mother insisted it was time to have our own house, and that made me hate the idea even more.

I remember when we started looking for new houses to buy. I can remember in full detail the day we went to look at the barn-red-colored house with no garage, on a quiet street that felt very far away from Grandpa's house. That house was only about three miles away, but it felt like it was in another country. I remember my mother talking about us living "alone" without Grandma and Grandpa, and I could not believe she could think that way. They were so good to all of us. I hated that house from the day we stepped in to see it. I hated the color, the smell, even the shape. I hated that an old lady lived and died there. I heard her name once, and I still remember it—Mrs. Clawson. I thought if we could just look a little bit more, surely there would be something better, newer, nicer, brighter. I begged and pleaded to stay at Grandpa's house, but it was to no avail. What was wrong with the house my father was born in? It was white. It was familiar. It was warm in the winter and cool in the summer. It was safe. We were together in it. What else could we want or need? My thoughts about where we should live were ignored. House shopping was on, and we were dragged to see them all, but I do not know why they bothered to bring us because our opinions did not matter. They bought that barn-red house. It was old and ugly and unbearably hot in the summer and freezing cold in the winter, and it always felt crowded, though there were fewer of us living there. Gone was my safe place with Grandpa and Grandma at night. Gone was the comfort of air-conditioning on hot summer nights. Gone were the sweet snacks Grandma gave me during the day and the salty ones Grandpa shared while we watched TV together at night. Gone was my best friend Dianne and playing with her and Honey every day after school and most weekends. Now what was I going to do? I hated that new, old house. I could not understand why no one would listen to me, and I just knew that moving into it was going to change everything.

Chapter 4

Change

We were all moved in, and I hated to be home. My parents tried to appease me with certain things, but nothing worked. My father customized and finished the attic for us, but I hated the sky-blue color of it with its sloping ceilings. I hated the spiral curved, maroon marbly looking stairs I had to walk up to get there. It was supposed to be this "cool bedroom" complete with a built-in platform bed my dad made. To me, it was still just an attic—cold in the winter, sticky-hot in the summer, and scary all year round. I had no interest at all in that platform bed or the stereo he bought and attached to it. I hated it. I missed sleeping comfortably and safe between my grandparents. Sometimes, after church on Sunday nights, we had to be up there in that attic bedroom all alone while my parents went to the diner. We were supposed to go to sleep because it was a school night, but I was terrified and wide awake with fear. It made me react to every thought I had and every sound I heard until the sweet sound of their voices walking in the door soothed my anxiety. I remember always having trouble sleeping. My mother used to force me to bed too early, and I would lie there listening to every sound for hours before tiring out. Everything was different there in that house, and everything was bad. The saving grace was that we got to see Grandma and Grandpa almost every weekend. A lot of times, that meant I could play with Dianne. Other times, Grandpa would pick us up and take us to the mall, or to department stores "in Joiseee," and we got to pick dinner at the fast-food place of our choosing. I tried to sleep over at Grandpa's as much as I could, but I usually had to go back home. At home, my father's presence was being felt less and less, and he worked more and more to afford that new home.

My sister Jodi used to love to get home after school, change into her pajamas, sit on the couch, and watch her favorite shows on TV. That was not me at all. I did not like to sit still for a long time, so I avoided being home as much as possible. I still am not really good at sitting and watching anything without a book, a magazine, a laptop, or my iPhone close. I usually have to be busy doing more than one thing at a time.

In elementary school, I was involved in every possible activity, encouraged by my mother to do so. In first grade, I was chosen to tutor kindergarten kids in reading, and that set the pace for my elementary school days. Immediately after school, I would go to the corner store, get an ice cream or some chips, walk five blocks home, and change my clothes to rush outside to play Wiffle ball, kickball or basketball. I would play whatever anyone was playing with whoever was there from the neighborhood. Often, I played until dusk or until I heard my name loudly echoing through the streets to come in. Homework was done with ease, so I always had time to play. Spelling bees, essay contests, and storytelling contests were part of my school routine. My teachers and my mother pushed me to compete because they knew I could do it and win. I even ran for class president more than once. Though I did not win, teachers I did not even know commented on how well my speech was and that I spoke very well in public. They had no idea how I did not sleep or eat the night before or the whole day until it was over. They had no idea that I was sweating and shaking and regretting every minute of it, whether I prevailed or not.

In the summer, I was out on the streets playing all day long. We had no air-conditioning in that ugly red house, so on hot summer nights, Dad and I would get in his car, crank up the air conditioner and ride around listening to the New York Mets play baseball on the radio. Sometimes we would drive to Port Richmond to get a famous

Ralph's Italian Ice, but most times, we had no destination. Those times were so special, and they lasted straight through the summer every year of elementary school.

Since church and family was a major part of my life, I was starting to become very close to a second cousin of mine, Yvonne. She was a little bit older and smarter than me, and I used to love to play with her and have her teach me some of what she was studying in school. She was a straight A student purist, who was extremely conscientious about doing her school and homework. As a child in middle school, she was one of my best friends. We could relate on almost every level, and she was even able to teach me things that were advanced for my age. She knew what it was to grow up as an Italian, non-Catholic, church girl with her parents very involved in ministry. I used to love sleeping over at her house since she lived near a little patch of woods, a perfect place for our imaginations to germinate. We would come in from the woods to a nice dinner her mother had made and then take turns showering. I loved washing my hair there because I got to choose from the many different good-smelling shampoos and conditioners I would always see advertised on TV. My mother always explained that they were too expensive for us to buy, and there was no reasoning with her, so I gave up asking. After showering, I could barely wait to eat all the delicious junk food we could from their pantry that seemed to demand my attention. Yvonne's mother kept it very well stocked. It was extra special for me because we never had a pantry stocked with good junk at our boring red home. Yvonne was always super skinny, and the TV shows and specials were much more exciting to her than the various types of chips and boxed sweet treats that were in abundance in that pantry. I loved to chew those packaged sweets slowly and savor every bite as I swallowed while being engrossed in TV on the parlor floor next to Yvonne and her mixed mutt Ginger.

Yvonne was an exceptionally fast reader. She introduced me to some of the wonderful novels for adolescent girls on the shelves written by great authors, like Judy Blume and Daniele Steele. We sometimes would read together, and she would highlight the most exciting parts, making them so much more vivid than they already were. Those times with Yvonne and her younger sisters tagging along are still some of my favorite childhood memories.

If I was home on the weekends, I kept to myself. I loved my friends and socializing, but I was okay with being alone too. I always found things to do if my small supply of reading was exhausted, like playing with my dolls and using my mind to create adventures where I could do whatever I wanted to by myself. I did not have to worry about being made fun of or saying something wrong, and I recall that feeling that I could do or be anything or anyone. I had an amazing imagination. My dreams of bigger and better things were always alive inside me. I believed all that I dreamed would come true. Most kids do; otherwise, why dream at all?

28

Chapter 5

French Kissing

It was around the time I was hanging out with Yvonne that I learned a lot about French kissing. That was not because we had the opportunity to do it but because we were reading a lot and watching kids at school and curiously learning like most adolescents. Some of this learning was from going to an occasional birthday party of friends from school where the typical party games were played like spin the bottle and seven minutes in heaven. I was never interested in doing anything at those parties, mostly because I was horrifically intimidated and insecure, but it was fun to watch everyone else.

Years later, I realized that I never really enjoyed kissing. In fact, I used to hate French kissing. I told guys that very thing in high school, after high school, even when I got a little older in college. In fact, I said that wherever and whenever it was necessary to let someone know. I just never really could explain why. I said I was bad at it, and I really felt that way, but that was not it at all. It took a lot of years to realize that intimate kissing is a beautiful thing with the right person, at the right time, in the right relationship. I had to face the reality of some things in my past. I had to confront them and call them what they were—*potentially devastating, disgusting, and wrong*. It took many years for me to get here, most of my life. I had to remember exactly why I hated the most beautiful kind of intimate kissing there is.

*****

"Lift up your shirt, Chince. Let's see how much you grew."

Chince, short for the Italian pronunciation of my name, spelled *Cintia* and pronounced, 'chin-see-ah,' was what he called me to make our relationship even more "special." He was the new youth pastor, a newlywed complete with a pregnant wife. They were from New England. His name was George. I could not have been more than nine or ten when it started. It was summer. I know because I was always with my dad in the summer, and he was usually very busy in the church office all day, and so was George. By nature, I am pretty private. I struggled with always being the chubby kid, and that just fed my reclusive nature, especially around other kids. I always felt different. I was always precocious—too smart for my grade, too aware of adult issues, and too developed physically for my age. I was the youngest in my classes too, since my birthday was in December. I started kindergarten at four years old, not five like everyone else. Anyway, I guess I was starving for affection, but you would never know it because I was careful not to ask for it. I never really wanted attention from anyone except my dad or my grandpa or my uncles, and it is not like I didn't get it, I did. I just wanted more. I remember how busy they were with the explosive church growth and multiple outreach projects in the summer. There were constant projects, like radio programs, building expansion plans, youth camps, children's productions, and so much other ministry outside of the walls of the church. I loved the activity in and outside of church. It was always exciting and it kept everyone busy.

For some reason, I have always related better to men. I used to beg and plead to go anywhere and do anything with my father or my grandfather. Sometimes, I even kind of regretted it because I got stuck on a carpentry job with my dad all day or stuck standing in one spot for hours at the mall with my grandpa, waiting for my sister and grandma to come back from actual shopping. It was my choice to do those things because I always felt more comfortable being with them. For a long time, I argued that I think more like a man. I feel more like a man, and I do not really need what women typically need. I also realized that I do not get offended at stereotypical male thinking or the male ego. Although true to a degree, I am a woman inside and out, and maybe part of what I endured made me want to mask my femininity for a while.

I am still pretty quiet about letting the people I love know when I need attention if they aren't already supplying it. In general, I am a better caregiver than recipient. Giving is just my nature. I am glad for it. It has opened the doors for reciprocity in every area of my life.

"*Here?!*" I shyly and nervously asked. *Not again,* I thought as my heart began to pound and my body began to tremble. We were on the back staircase in the old church. I remember the mint-green-colored paint that covered the cinder block walls of the stairwell and the fear I felt that my father or grandfather might see us.

"*Yes, here, Chince, fast. No one will know. I will protect you. I can't wait to see how big you're getting.*"

I felt so scared, so strange. Why did he care about me? But at the same time, he was good at flashing the right nod or convincing wink that made me feel special. He had a way of getting me to do whatever he wanted. He had a way of making me feel like I was his. At that young age, I saw him as fun and handsome, and he treated me like a real person, not just some dumb kid. Not like his bossy wife who talked to me like I was any other dumb kid, because I wasn't. Didn't she know? I was *special.* So special to him, he said it all the time, even though he usually had to beg and convince me to do what he wanted in the mint-green-colored stairwell; in the old, falling-apart, forest-green 1970-something Chevrolet Caprice; in his taupe-colored church office; in his new snow-white second-floor apartment that he shared with his wife and infant son and the kitchen towels with the little strawberries on them neatly draped over the handle of the oven in that tiny kitchenette.

*****

Being touched in a sexual way as a child, I did not even understand what was happening. I mean I knew when my skin was stroked by a finger that it felt good. I mean, I thought it felt good, but there was just something a little off, and I could not process exactly what that was because I was so innocent. I did not have the good, grown-up, common sense to know what was wrong; but somehow I knew it was wrong, and along with that came the guilt and fear. I heard cunning things like, *"This is between me and you,"* and *"It's our little secret,"* and, *"You can tell me anything, you are very, very special to me."* And that is when I decided to just go with it and welcome it and try to just believe it was all okay. I mean, what choice did I have? I remember the warnings, *"This is just between us, you cannot talk about it, it is private, and you will get in big trouble."* I had no way of knowing at the time that I was with a skilled predator—a freak of nature—and I could never say no. He would not hear of it. He knew how to turn my no's, my fears, and my guilt into whatever he wanted.

Parents think they know everything about what is up with their kids, but most of them are just plain clueless, especially back then. No cell phones. No laptops. No GPS. No education for parents and kids about right and wrong touching and right and wrong relationships. And no one wants to believe that preachers can be pedophiles just like any other Joe. No one wants to believe that even a young, promising preacher being mentored by your own, kind, truly God-fearing father is a deviant animal. These are people with iron-seared consciences. They are predators; wolves in sheep's clothing. They are monsters.

*****

This couple was a big part of our lives. Our barn-red house was walking distance from their apartment, and my parents treated them like family. After all, they had moved to Staten Island, far from their parents and her siblings, to be youth pastors in our church, and his parents had long been members of the church organization we were a part of. We were, for all intents and purposes, family. We shared many meals, and they were often with us at Uncle Joe's.

The first time I went to their apartment with my family, his wife made delicious Chicken Kiev. The butter dripped down my chin when I bit into it, and it was yummy. My father and George laughed over that dinner, talking about sports and church, while my sister and I took turns checking on his sleeping infant. I pretended that I was his secret wife and that their baby was really my baby. It was a nice escape. That story felt good. His wife asked for me to visit again to keep an eye on the baby while she went downstairs to do laundry. I was excited to visit, knowing his wife would be there close, to prevent the secret stuff from happening. I should have been smart enough to realize he would make it happen somehow.

"Honey, I'm going to do the laundry," she said to him, white laundry basket in hand, in that awful Boston-based accent of hers. I felt the blood drain out of me. *Please don't leave,* I thought.

"Keep an eye on the baby, Cynthia," she said louder to me, walking down the stairs and on her way out of the apartment. *"I love you honey,"* to him.

"I love you too," he said, his voice high pitched and excited as the downstairs door closed loudly. I knew the excitement was for me, and I thought I knew what was coming next. I was right, and it was too late. I was trapped. This would be worse than before. We were *really* alone.

Revealing his naked body to me at nine years of age was something I cannot really put in to words. One time, before this, he made me touch him in the mall while we were shopping with my father who was in another aisle close by. He insisted that we were *"best buddies,"* and it was *"OK."* I felt so terrified! I did not want this. I was ashamed. I was being bad. It was wrong. He laughed and joked and teased me for being scared. I wanted to tell my grandfather and my father so badly, but I just could not do it. I even wanted to tell Yvonne, and I remember trying so hard to get her to talk about it but never actually getting there. I was so afraid to get in trouble. I was told this was *"our secret"* and that everyone would be very mad at me. The feelings are all still very real, and the scenes are very clear in my mind. At that point, I did not understand any of it, and it was really terrifying and confusing, but I made it all go away whenever he was not around. The only problem was, he was always around.

Chapter 6

Negativity

There are enough people against us in life. They are negative. They are antagonistic. They do not want us to succeed. For this reason alone, do not be negative toward yourself. Small-minded people belittle others with rude comments and behavior that is not conducive to a positive environment. Though motivation for this behavior may be varied, the outcome is the same, and it can be devastating to us. Stay away from negative people. Stay away from small-minded people. Be bigger than them. It sounds so simple, yet it is extremely profound, as these kinds of people surround us every day, and their negativity can affect us. Even more importantly, do not be this kind of person.

There was a study done by a well-known psychologist named John Gottman. He and his team took years to study people and how negative comments affect their performance in work environments. What the researchers concluded was that the number of positive comments it takes to outweigh one negative comment is five. Five to one. This was based on data collected in different environments over a long time. Other experts believe the ratio is more likely twenty to one. The effect of this theory is physiological. The prefrontal cortex of the brain shuts down when fear is instilled in someone. The sympathetic nervous system becomes engaged, and the ability to think shuts down, almost like in fight or flight during a stressful situation.

If this theory holds true in the work environment, how true is it in school or in a social situation, and in every minute of every day of our busy lives? When I first heard about this study and the outcomes, I remember thinking, five comments that are positive are necessary just to cancel out the one negative. How many more positive comments do we need to perform well? How much more positivity do we need to stay on top? If you do the math over a short lifespan— the negative numbers are huge! We need to make up the difference ourselves and speak positive words over ourselves *daily*. This is more necessary than we believe, and though it begins with a positive way of thinking, we need to speak out positive words to ourselves every day to counter every negative word we have ever spoken or heard spoken over us. We need to build ourselves up and build up those around us. We need to build up, not tear down.

*****

Standing in his apartment near mirrored tiles on the dining room wall, for the first time he made me undress completely. I was mortified, and I was trapped. I tried to refuse, and he smiled and coaxed and pleaded and teased with a dry mouth, watching until I did. He told me I didn't have to, but he didn't mean it. He just had a way to make me do what he wanted while I smiled and laughed with him. I do not know what feeling scared me the most—my chubby, imperfect, adolescent body being revealed; the terror of her walking in; or him touching me again and again, forcing his thick, dry, disgusting tongue in my mouth and exploring my body wherever and however he chose. I was trapped. I hated his tongue, God knows how much I hated it! I still do. It is harder to remember this day than anyone will ever know…

God, please don't let her get here too soon, was the beginning of my thoughts. *God, please don't let him hurt me too much*. He kept asking if his touch felt good and if I liked it, and he wanted me to tell him it felt good. But it did not. I didn't want him mad at me, so I pretended it was all okay. *I was special. I tried to convince myself.* Yuck. Ouch. Ewww. *God, please let this end fast.* I had no idea what sex or sexual feelings were at the time. I had no idea what good sexual feelings were. *Sex* was a foreign word that my friends and I joked about. It was a subject unknown, and we were content with that because *that* was normal. Why did I have to learn this now? I did not want to, but I was trapped. It was too late. I was so stupid to think I could visit there in his home alone and *not* be his *special* friend. It was the dumbest idea ever.

*****

I spent as much time as I could with my father, but he was always very busy. Busy with the church, busy with his carpentry business, busy helping Uncle Joe with construction, busy helping everyone he could, and busy being everything he could be. I wanted my dad to know so bad what was happening, but I was so afraid to displease him or for him not to believe me or that I would get in trouble, the way George said I would. I do not resent my father being busy at all. He was always bringing me with him to the church, and while he was running around working in all parts of the church, George was on the prowl, cornering me somewhere. It may be difficult to understand that any attention – even from a "George" is welcomed to an innocent child whose family's lives are hectic with everyday life. I always understood my father's drive and passion, and I did my best to be a part of it. My dad's drive and passion for God and life have taught me about God and life. His love is so constant and covering, it has allowed me to understand the true, unrelenting, incomparable, unconditional, perfect love of God. It simply was not possible to be seen and protected 24/7 by my busy father, and I could not bring myself to tell him what was happening even though I wished he could stop it and rescue me and make it all go away.

Telling my mother was not an option either. For one thing, I spent most of my time with my grandparents and my father as a little girl. Although I love her and respect her, we never really connected when I was a child. It was difficult for me to talk to her about anything that really mattered to me. I always felt she was loud and inappropriate, and although I loved her, I knew I was different than

36

her. She was bubbly and impulsive and wanted to be the center of attention. I was quiet, calculated, and happy to be in the corner of the room. I was a thinker, slow to speak. I was patient to learn about what interested me, trying my best to perfect it with the help of any expert willing to assist. She was easily entertained in a social setting, enjoying the attention, which I shunned. I remember not wanting my friends around her because she was so loud and jovial, and I was afraid she would embarrass them. I now know that my friends appreciated her fun-loving nature and welcomed her warmth. She made them feel at ease. Somehow, as a child, I felt that she was too busy talking to really listen to me. My mother always liked to go to bed early, and although her late was not really late, she refused to let me "break a rule" and stay up later at night, thinking I just wanted my own way. I really could not sleep because I wasn't tired. My mother liked silly TV shows and shopping. I liked reading and sports and learning about different arts and sciences. We were different, and it was just something I knew.

She threw me a surprise party once. I had warned her not to do it, but she did not hear me. I was in middle school—the time of life when kids are transitioning into adolescence, loathing their own bodies, looking for acceptance, and experimenting with new things. Aside from the fact that I had raging hormones, conflict in everything I did, and challenges in our family, which seemed to be falling apart, I was leaning toward being rebellious and did not want my friends near her or anyone else in my family. I preferred hanging out with them alone and doing whatever they wanted to do. I walked through the front door, and much to my horror, she was standing in the middle of many of my friends screaming, "SURPRISE!" with a big smile. I froze, rolled my eyes, made a not-so-happy face, and then walked to the dining room. The dining room table had a big cake and some snacks and some party plates and cups, and I was so mad. I glared at her with an "I asked you *not* to do this" look and told my friends to get their coats and that we should go for a walk. At that moment, I was frightened that someone would see my home and my life as weird, and I was very angry that she did not listen to me when I begged her not to throw a party for me. She was calling my name, softly at first and then firmly. Then she called my first and middle name (you know how mothers do this), but I kept walking out the door with my friends. She crossed the line. I did not want a party. I hated to be the center of attention.

It was the end of December, a freezing cold afternoon that was quickly turning into night, and we were walking and talking, seeing our breath with bright, red noses and cold hands and feet that were avoiding slipping on black ice on the streets. My friends decided we should walk to a store where they knew we could buy some beer and we would drink it down fast, hoping it would warm us up until we had to walk back home. I knew I hurt my mother, and I knew she meant well, but I did not want what she wanted. Why couldn't she understand? I just wanted her to listen to me. Arriving at the door late that night, freezing and full of guilt, I saw her sitting on the stairs in tears. She was mad at me but also really hurt. This party was more about her and how she wanted to please me, and I knew I had really hurt her, but being a preteen, I didn't know how to resolve it. I was shoving popcorn down my throat to erase the alcohol smell that was on my lips as I listened to her tearful speech about how everything was for me and how much I hurt her. With a true feeling of sadness, I tried to apologize, but I was afraid because she was mad too. Somehow, I made it to my bed without a scratch. Ahhhh, the feeling of my bed! It felt so good that night. I was tired and cold from walking so much and a little dizzy from the beer that I had never had before, which was sitting in an empty stomach. The beer was new for me and so exciting because no one knew we drank it, and that felt liberating.

Deep down inside, I was even surer that I needed to stay close to my father. He was getting home really late, working as a pastor and a carpenter in order to provide for us while still following his calling in life without compensation. I noticed him coming home later and my parents speaking less and less. I was so focused on making my father happy. I never gave him trouble. I remember tiptoeing down those old creaky stairs at night, careful not to let my mother hear me, to watch TV with my dad. He was and still is an avid sports fan, so it was usually the Mets or the Knicks or the Giants or the Rangers, depending on the season.

My maternal grandfather, Sergifreddo (Fred), was a first-generation immigrant from Italy, and he was scary and mean. He spoke only Italian, and if he needed to, he could spew out some angry, broken English. We hated to drive 350 miles to visit them on Christmas break and sometimes for Memorial Day or the Fourth of July, leaving Grandma Rose and Grandpa Joe and Daddy's family there celebrating in Staten Island without us. The house in Ohio was old and dirty, and it smelled old and dirty. We avoided mean old Grandpa Fred at all costs, in sharp contrast to wanting to be with Grandpa Joe doing whatever he was doing. My maternal grandmother, Lena, was simple and oh so sweet. She had a modest vocabulary mostly used to demonstrate kindness and love to her family. Her laugh was distinctive and infectious, and we heard it often. She loved to cook and she loved to eat. She loved church, and she loved her five children. Her husband never liked the fact that she loved her new found charismatic, non-Catholic Christian church. It was a conservative, family-oriented Assembly of God that placed an emphasis on understanding God's desire for families to love Him and each other. Grandpa Fred called it too radical, as he remained a committed Catholic who never went to church. On cold, snowy days in Ohio, Grandma Lena would take her five children with her to church alone, sometimes coming home to a locked door. Grandpa Sergifreddo would punish her for going to church and only unlock the door to let her and the children in when he was ready for her to make a meal for him. I did not know my Grandpa Sergifreddo at all. I was afraid of him and could not really communicate with him. I did not really know my Grandma Lena so well either as a child, because she lived so far away. I remember that I loved her very unique version of wedding soup. It was a chicken-based broth with delicious little veal meatballs that were full of an overly generous amount of imported grated Romano cheese, eggs, and black pepper. It took a long time to make those meatballs so perfectly round and tiny between two palms that delicately went circular in opposite directions. They were so succulent and soft, and they puffed so perfectly in that rich and flavorful broth that was slow cooked all day and then clarified to perfection. Our mouths watered as those petite meatball marvels were carefully spooned into a beautiful white porcelain soup tureen—one of the few decorative pieces of serveware Grandma had. Once the broth was in that giant bowl, layers of crusty, day-old semolina bread, and pro-volone cheese followed. When it was full to the tippy top, that heavy lid covered this modest, but so hearty, coveted family recipe for about thirty minutes. Not too long after, when all those flavors married, we sat around talking, laughing, slurping, and swallowing, the meatballs melting in our mouths, the bread becoming one with that buttery cheese—a true tradition of my mother's family. Much later in life, after her husband and eldest son died and her neighborhood deteri-orated, life became really difficult for Grandma Lena. Her children and their families were far away and spread out across the country, and money was virtually nonexistent. Together, her children agreed that she move in with my mother in Staten Island, New York. It was then that my sisters and I got to know her really well and realize just how great she was. In fact, it was at that time that Grandma Lena taught me the secret of how to make those delicious veal meatballs in that delicious broth.

"The secret is lots of eggs, a whole lot more grated Romano cheese, black pepper, and nothing else!" she explained. *"And never ever use breadcrumbs, onions, or garlic! You want the meatballs tender and puffed, so you have to roll them very tiny. If you want, you could finely chop some fresh Italian parsley, but just add a small amount so as not to change the distinct flavors."*

Grandma joining my mother was a really good thing for Mom too. They had a lot of time to bond and laugh and share, and my mother felt honored to give back to her mother in the end of her life.

Life for me went on in church and school, and George was still on the prowl. He was so beyond obsessed with giving in to his hellish desires and satisfying his out-of-control flesh that he seemed to have no fear of consequences. The church office space consisted of a row of equally sized square offices up the left side of a narrow, rectangular hallway. The offices were set up for ministry staff in this order: church secretary, pastor (my dad), assistant pastor, outreach ministry, a closet for office supplies, music minister, and George had the last one. One workday in the middle of the summer, when I was spending the day with my dad at the church, George "invited" me to his office. As usual, everything happened so fast that I could hardly recognize the pattern and was trapped before I could escape. Although I was precocious, I was probably around eleven years old. Somehow, he managed to con me into lying down on the floor of his office, locking the door. He laid me down and had me completely naked, freezing and frightened to death while he jested at me and laughed with sheer delight.

"Wow, Chince, you're really growing!" he panted, eyes wide, mouth dry. I was sick to my stomach for every reason I can remember, not the least of which was his terrible tongue.

In the following few moments of disgust, I was startled and paralyzed, listening to the music minister abruptly knock on the door. Trying the handle and noticing it was locked, he called out in his familiar and distinct, Cuban American accent, *"Ay, George, you in there, bro? You know your door is locked?"* Fear welled up inside, and I was ice-cold and shaking, holding my breath in silence while George cleared his aroused throat.

"Oh really? It's locked? Just studying, give me a minute. Be out in a minute," he called. To me, very quietly, he said, *"Hahahaha… Aw, Chince…calm down! Heeheeheehee…it's fine. Relax! Hahahaha,"* he taunted as I jumped up, frantically getting dressed and feeling so angry and confused while George continued to laugh mockingly at me like I was a fool, zipping his pants. I ran under his desk as he opened his door. Disaster expertly averted again for him.

I do not remember how I got out of there unnoticed by the music minister, but I know that somehow I did. I made a mental note to stay far away from that office at the end of the hall, feeling the churning in my sour stomach all day until I was out of there and safe at home.

There was incident after incident, anywhere and everywhere until I was numbed by it all in an effort to cope. I turned the pain and fear into excitement. George had no fear, and he was always around. My dad would take me to church early with him, and we would pick up George. My dad would take me to the mall or a department store, and George would be there and he would try to expose himself to me in public with my father just a few feet away. As terrifying as it was, it was also exciting. All the attention seemed to be on me, and the constant flirtation with danger was exhilarating. At eleven years old, I was being taught dangerous patterns of behavior and was so confused with no one to talk to because this was *"our little secret,"* and I would be in big trouble if I spoke.

There was incident after incident in setting after setting. Then one day, in what seemed like an out-of-the-blue move, that assistant pastor and his enabling wife and the baby were on their way back to New England. Rumor had it that he made his way through a lot of young girls and there was a lot of hoopla about it for a while. I even remember the new music minister commenting when accusations flew about him saying, *"Oh, no, again? Wasn't that the accusation in the last church?"* Apparently, that comment fell on deaf ears. George stole the innocent childhood of too many young girls as easily as a skilled thief robs a bank, never looking back.

One of those young girls wound up "going too far" with her boyfriend because she "could not stop." The new raindrops of feelings George introduced to her became a raging waterfall that ended up with her getting pregnant by her young boyfriend. All I really know about that time is that he vehemently denied every accusation over and over and over again to my father and grandfather. (I learned this many years later.) I am not really sure about a lot, including why the church board decided to handle (or not handle) things the way they did. I do not really care either. I just knew he was gone.

The crazy thing is, I missed him. I have since learned that you cannot really know the implications of a situation like I experienced until you actually face it as an adult in order to understand the dynamics of what happened. You also learn much later that it was not your fault at all. Although this sounds so simple to know, there is a nagging, relentless voice that tries to follow you and impose blame on you for things you are not guilty of at all. Perfect love from God quiets those voices, canceling the fear and shame they are attached with, subtly revealing the truth of that horrible experience.

I missed George when he left. I saw him every so often because he was still involved in the church organization. He made it through some very grueling questioning and accusations and convinced the new organization he became affiliated with that he was a true man of God and that he had no reason to repent because he never did anything he was accused of. And sadly, he never changed. On special occasions, when he visited our church or at a large convention, he would take every opportunity to be alone with me, even if just for a look or a touch, and many times he succeeded (though they were few and far between). This "attraction" he had for me and the whole situation was more damaging than I ever thought it could be. I tried desperately to cope with it and not permit it to affect me, but its effects were far reaching. Part of the impact it had was that it unleashed the precocious hormonal adolescent from within me way too soon. It forced me to feel feelings I should not have felt for years to come. God's grace and the convictions I had to honor Him prevented a lot of what might have beens. This terribly sad occurrence in my life caused me to fear and to constantly look over my shoulder. I suffered from terrible guilt most of the time and worried that someone would find out and that I would be punished harshly. It stole my innocence and robbed me of my dignity. It taught me to self-loathe and to feel shame on a regular basis. It made me want to always be covered and, as many people have surmised, probably forced me to stay overweight, using food as comfort and fat as protection from letting anyone get too close. This "attraction" he had toward me and many other innocent young girls was a subtle, demonic, controlling power that takes over for a long time—until you take authority over it and stop it.

Chapter 7

Forensic Medicine

"Forensic medicine." I did not even know that was what it was called, but oh, how I loved the programs on television! I watched with imagination. I dreamed with confidence that one day I would be the one to figure out why someone died and how they died, and I would be the hero, proud to report my findings. I would develop new medicines and maybe even help develop new vaccines. I would dedicate my life to curing, maybe even wiping out diseases and preventing infectious pandemics and epidemics from destroying towns and cities.

I was obsessed with human anatomy. It was never just eyes and arms and hearts and ears—I was always so fascinated with the human body and how it works. I still am. How does the ear hear? How can the eye see? I started copying heart and eye and ear anatomy out of books onto poster paper to color and label for fun. I brought them to my teachers for extra credit. Some of my teachers appreciated my enthusiasm while others politely refused them and continued in their monotonous tones. I understood, and I felt a little sorry for them. Then again, why should they be excited? They were stuck there all day with a lot of kids much less motivated than me. *Poor teachers,* I thought. *I will be out of here in no time and they are still stuck. I'm going to be a doctor.*

*****

My father was always a student of the Bible with a heart to help people, but more than that, he was called to preach and teach and pastor and to touch the world. To do this right, you not only have to be a lover of God but also a lover of people. My dad began to realize more and more that the God he served with so much vigor was a good God who took pleasure in giving good gifts to His children. He began to listen to preachers who believed the same basic doctrines, but with new insight. He was understanding more and more that a blood covenant provided the avenue for us to approach a Heavenly God without guilt or shame. My father began to boldly preach that healing and prosperity are promised through the cross and that God would honor His Word.

What is interesting about my father was that he began studying much of these principles out of anger in an attempt to disprove them. The deeper he dug, the clearer it was.

The traditional church he was in began to make waves at what he was teaching. The board members held weekly meetings, and the subject of the pastor preaching "heresy" became a constant topic. The more my dad preached it, the more the congregation grew, and the more the board fought and demanded he stop. They encouraged my father to resign as the pastor of that church, which had tripled in growth and was thriving since his leadership of just a few years. It was not his desire to cause a problem or split the church. He simply could no longer compromise this message of God's goodness and our ability to trust in it. My grandfather and most of the family questioned his leaving and became angry that he would break tradition. They pulled away from my dad and stopped speaking to him, but Dad was fully persuaded and followed the conviction in his heart. He believed God called him to do this, and He trusted that it would all work out. It made me want to be more like him than ever. I was also sure I wanted to be there with him. The only problem was, I was not there with him, and I had to figure out how I could be.

I had been fighting with my mother more and more, and my grades began to slip. As I said, my mother was great at pushing me to do well academically. She was responsible for making me study spelling and reading and writing and was the reason I actually won the schoolwide storytelling contest one year and was entered in the city-wide competition. She was the reason I was awarded certificates from the National Honor Society and National French Honor Society and why I was on the dean's list and helping out in the dean's office. She was proud of my accomplishments, but I was starting to get tired of studying because of the changes at home and in my adolescent body. I was going to the park instead of school, praying I would never be caught, and most times I got away with it. I was smart enough to keep up in school, though I was not excelling as I had been. It did not take long before I was visiting the dean for punishment instead of working for him.

One day my mother looked me in the eye as she got ready to go to work (a new thing for all of us—her working) and told me my father left and he did not want to hear from us. I was sitting in front of the picture window in the back of the house, in the kitchen. At one end of the kitchen was the tiny half bathroom my mother used to put her makeup on. The window was next to the bathroom. This window had quite a few glass shelves, and they housed a variety of plants in different stages of growth. She called it the Florida window, and she loved it so much. My mother was always really good at planting and growing things. She had a green thumb, loving her plants, herbs, flowers and vegetables, talking to and caring for them daily. She could grow anything. She paid a lot of attention to them, and it showed. I hated the window and all the plants. I did not like the dirt and the bugs that came with the plants, and I thought they required a little bit too much work. That afternoon, I sat in front of that Florida window, watching her finish her makeup, thinking about what I would do with the information she just threw at me. I hated listening to her tell me I could not call my father, and I began to get angry. I could feel the anger boiling inside of me because I knew he would never say that or want that—at least I thought I knew. I also knew there was more to the story than "he just left." I knew his love for us, and I knew she was leaving for work soon, so I temporarily bottled up my anger, went up to my room, and began to pack. There was no way I was staying there another day.

When I heard her door close and the car start up and pull away, I went to the phone to call my father at his office. I had packed a bag, and I was ready to go anywhere but home. I fantasized about becoming homeless or moving in with someone who wanted me or even doing Lord knows what to get away from there. I just wanted out, and I wanted a bit of peace from what had suddenly become a mixed-up life. Before I ran away, I thought it only polite to at least inform my father, even if he did not want me. With my mother away at work, I dialed his number to tell him I loved him and that I would keep in touch. He deserved that. I was able to talk to him immediately. His voice was strong, kind, welcoming, and familiar, and I felt a flicker of happiness inside. I told him I was leaving the house. I told him I was tired of my life and that I wanted to be bad. He listened intently, then I could hear him smile and say, *"Are you ready to get your heart right with God?"*

Tears immediately streamed down my face as I listened to his prompts, *"Hmmm? Honey? Are you ready?"*

"But, Dad, I don't want to be here. I want to be with you," I said, trying to stop my voice from breaking, unsuccessfully.

"So then ask the Lord, and believe it, and it will happen. God is faithful. Everything will be okay, honey."

We prayed a simple prayer and I felt a release inside of me. My father told me he would come and see me soon and that he would bring me a new Bible and a lot of things to listen to and read. As promised, he brought those items the very next day. I began to read about how to pray in faith and speak positive and trust that God heard me when I prayed and that I could have the desires of my heart. I learned to stretch my faith and trust God beyond what I saw and felt in order to live with my dad. I believed that nothing was impossible. I learned to be more obedient and submissive to my mother and to speak what I wanted and it would happen. So every day, several times throughout the day, I would say out loud to myself,

Thank you, Father God, that I am going to live with my father at 204 Sunwell Avenue. I will go to T-ville High School and will live with my father. Thank you that my mother will agree and it will be easy.

At times, if I mentioned this to my mother, she would laugh and say it was impossible and that I could not live with him. But I would walk away and say under my breath that I would live with my dad because God was good and He would give me my heart's desire. I was confident that my God would honor my heartfelt cry of faith, against all opposition. All the while at home with my mother I tried to do my best at school. I tried to be happy and more polite. I tried to be who I knew I should but I knew I wanted to be somewhere else.

The school year was winding down and summer was rapidly approaching. My room began to feel stifling hot in midday. It was May and exceptionally warm. I was home alone after school, downstairs in the ugly basement of that ugly red house. I was probably looking for a game or a toy that was stored on a bunch of old shelves at the bottom of the stairs. Or maybe I was getting clothes out of the washer. Whatever it was, I remember the loud, invasive ring of the old phone. It almost startled me. I moved quickly to answer it, mostly to stop the ringing. When I picked up the phone, I could hear my grandpa's voice, faint and cracking as he said my name, making sure it was me. His voice sounded so strange. Grandpa never sounded like this. He was crying like a child. I listened closely as he blurted out some of the worst news I ever heard, *"Uncle Joe died today, Cynthia. He had a heart attack."* His sobbing continually interrupted him, and I felt a little bit lost. Was he talking about my Uncle Joe who had recently moved to Florida? Uncle Joe who always made everyone laugh and made the pizzas and calzones after church on Sunday nights? Uncle Joe who always gave me hot peppers and laughed hysterically until he coughed? Was Grandpa actually giving me this horrible news? Was this real? What would I do? What do I say? I had no idea how to process this as a middle school child. Louder and a bit more firmly and almost yelling at me in his Brooklyn accent, he repeated, *"Cynthia, are you there? Did you hear me?"* He said it again, clearer and louder, but not overtly crying. *"Uncle Joe died of a harrhhhht attack today, call your fawhhtha. Tell him."* Before the phone clicked, I heard deep sobs that were just unimaginable. I was in shock, unsure of how to tell my dad; but without really thinking, I called him and I told him. I remember his shocked and sad reaction as I told him how Grandpa had called me and told me. He asked if anyone else was there, and I told him I was alone. I told him to come and get me so I could be with him and he said to ask if I could. I remember he pressed hold and one of the ladies helping him in the office came to the phone in tears, telling me to please stay with my dad and to protect him from all the angry people in that church who might show up at the wake and be disrespectful to my dad during this terrible moment in his life. I promised I would not leave his side. As the plans began to be made, I was allowed to be with my dad. I packed a small bag and brought a few dresses for the next few terrible days. We went to the wake together. I remember praying under my breath while walking by my father's side, arm in arm, staring directly into the face of everyone who approached or passed by. I would not even go to the restroom until my father made me, and I made him promise to stand outside the door and not leave until I returned. It was such a terrible time. I witnessed my cousins, grandparents, my Aunt Vera, and my dad experience one of the hardest things we ever had to deal with in our lives—at a time when my father was so isolated from everyone. I felt helpless with my aunt and cousins, but I was determined not to stop praying for a minute and to never leave my father's side. My father cried with me the night after the funeral. He told me that I was such a strength to him. I knew it was just the beginning of me being a strength at his side. It was a big part of my calling in life, and I felt honored and humbled.

I was propelled by my strength alongside my father through a very dark time. With the help of the God I knew well, even as young as I was, I continued to speak what I believed would be true every day throughout the rest of May and June. It had been at least six months since I began my young faith journey, and I had memorized a lot of scripture and had become familiar with many principles to live successfully and move in the direction I was supposed to. I was learning to be more respectful as I believed for what I wanted and stayed focused while behaving a bit better.

One day after the last day of the school year, my mother opened my bedroom door, peeked her head in, and very nonchalantly said, *"Call your father, tell him to come get you and go live with him."*

Although for a moment I doubted, I did not hesitate. It took me all of five minutes to obey her. I called my father, who first questioned if I was sure. Believing what I was praying for would happen, over the past few months, I had been stuffing my favorite things in large Hefty garbage bags and storing them under my bed so no one would notice. I called this putting action to my faith. In no time, my dad was in front of the red house, honking the horn; it had been less than an hour. I will never forget loading my garbage bags and my blissfully happy self into the maroon interior of his Cadillac that smelled delicious, like him, with the air conditioner washing away the heated discomfort of life as I knew it. My prayers were answered. I was saved and never ever going back. So, when it was time to transfer from one New York City Public High School to another, it was no problem, I could give up my friends for my dad. I moved into a basement apartment, sleeping on an itchy, pull-out couch with a mattress as thin as a yoga mat, in a tiny makeshift living room that it barely fit in. This was now "my room", and it was perfect.

That night, I slept like a baby—in cool comfort on that couch—happy as a clam. I loved that basement apartment and have a lot of memories of it. We stayed there for about a year, and I went to the high school I wanted to—alone and away from all my childhood friends. My new friends from church were a good replacement. Cindy B., my namesake friend from Bayonne, came over a lot. My dad would make us food, and we would giggle and eat and call older friends who drove to come pick us up and take us to the movies or bowling or for ices or whatever. I was loving life. And then, when it was time to move to New Jersey and go from New York City High School number two to New Jersey high school number three—it was no problem. I had hoped and believed it was possible to be with him, against odds, and it came true. I would follow my dad wherever he led me. Nothing else mattered except that I was with him—oh, and I was with him for good, *never to go back*. I was from him, for him, with him, headed for ministry, the happiest girl on earth. I was where I was supposed to be—of that I was sure.

As we crossed the Outerbridge from Staten Island to New Jersey for the last time only to go back for whatever may be, I thought about my role as a daughter. My dad was soooooo brave—the bravest man I knew! He broke family tradition to pursue what was in his heart, clinging only to his faith. He had support from no one in his family and just a few friends who believed in him. He left tradition and, *"Oh, what a horrible person he was,"* were the vicious rumors. But I knew better. Oh yes, I did! He was not just my dad. He was special. If you looked in his eyes, you knew it. You needed to trust his steps and that he was a person who would not settle. He shut out the loud static of the taunting angry naysayers and stayed focused on his call. I knew these things. He was my dad, but he was also a man of God. I could be his support. I would protect him. I would be the best daughter ever. That was the least I could do. He rescued me from a life of mediocrity, routine, and compromise. For that, I am ever grateful.

Chapter 8

Sacrifice

To obey is better than sacrifice. Christians seem to like to quote this in a prideful sort of way, and I think we miss the point. Do not get me wrong. I believe this principle, but I think one has to understand the context of how it was written to probe a bit deeper into it. In the Old Testament, a sacrifice was made to show your love, your devotion, your loyalty to your God. It was an act to demonstrate what was in your heart, but obedience was required to prove your true devotion. Often, people whose hearts were not pure would try to present precious gifts or money in lieu of obedience to no avail. The obedient heart is the point. What if you have a sacrificial heart of obedience? I mean, sometimes, a sacrifice is really difficult—like giving up your dreams for someone you love. If you think about it, aren't you obeying too? The point is, what is in your heart? A person with an obedient heart does not think about himself when he acts. His behavior, though it may be seen as sacrificial, is just the heart of love doing what comes as right. Sacrifice is a selfless act and so is total obedience. The focus is never about the person offering the sacrifice or complying with the obedience. The focus is on doing what is right, despite the cost.

The choices we make to please the people we love who are trying their best to guide us do not always appear to benefit us. If our hearts are pure about the decisions we make and we follow the path of obedience, sacrificing our own desires, sometimes the road to our destiny twists and turns and becomes longer than the proverbial straight and narrow. In the end, we will get there. The reward for living selfless will be greater than we could have imagined. We have to obey the still, small voice inside; and if we lose our way, we have to believe God will set us straight.

*****

We moved into a beautiful house in suburban New Jersey. It was the kind of home I thought we would never live in on a cul-de-sac in a really nice central New Jersey town. It was brand new, big and beautiful with a great yard and a built-in pool—simply amazing. I loved living with my dad in that house and going to church with him every Thursday night and Sunday morning. Life was so exciting, but it did not take long for me to realize that moving to suburban New Jersey was not everything that I had hoped for. I liked that I was a native New Yorker, and I did not want to lose my identity as such, but being anywhere with my father was just more important. I would follow him anywhere. He was my hero, my mentor, my friend. We always had a very special bond. We had the kind of relationship other kids envied. He told me once that he remembered dedicating me to God. He recalled that it was very special when he did it because it was private—just him and God, with tears in his eyes and a strong sense that God was there, listening closely. Dad and I were living in New Jersey in a great house, and I was going to high school there. I hated school. I could not connect with the snobby, upper-middle-class mentality that was now my life. I did not care to engage in the social network. I sacrificed my friends and the comfortable school life I knew to be with my dad, but it did not really feel like much of a sacrifice at all until it came to school. My body image was getting worse, and I started starving myself desperately trying to get skinny and look like the other girls. I would eat a slice of pizza or a half of a cheeseburger from McDonald's and throw it up. I was losing weight and damaging my stomach, but it was a cycle that I had trouble stopping. On the weekends, I was really binging and purging, stuffing myself with all kinds of junk food, then throwing up then laying down in a lot of pain and exhausted.

I was very plugged into church, the youth group, and all my friends from there. We spoke the same language. We had the same purpose. It was there that I really connected with John. I met him and his brother through one of the secretaries working at the church who was from Staten Island. I was shy and quiet when we met because I was immediately attracted to him and his blue eyes and the big brown beauty mark on his face that I wanted to reach out and touch. He was cute and funny and passionate about church. He was a lot like me, a Staten Island New York Italian-American who loved Jesus. He was very involved at church, working the soundboard at most services while learning it from the guy who put it all together. He was involved in the youth group, and he played basketball at school. We were in the same high school at one point before I moved to New Jersey. He was a senior, and I was a sophomore. He was always a lot of fun to be with because he had a good sense of humor and was pretty happy-go-lucky about life.

I liked him a lot from the first day I met him. He was so handsome with those sparkly blue eyes and that sweet brown beauty mark on his face. I had a major crush. John and I were forced into social situations a lot. We were asked to babysit for people's kids from church together so they could go to church functions. He was my ride to youth group each week and to lots of other places because I did not drive yet. We spent a lot of Friday nights at youth group together and a lot of Saturdays either setting up special staging or whatever was needed for a youth meeting or church event. We had mutual friends too, so it was not unusual for all of us to go bowling together or to a movie or just to go out for a pizza. Besides all that, I spent a lot of time with his mother. I thought she was really fun to be with. I liked her a lot. I saw her as a "cool mom," and she was always apt to bring me wherever she was going, often to their house just to hang out.

John and I were together a lot, and I remember that I always tried to be someone I wasn't to make him like me more. I think he secretly had a crush on my best friend at the time, Cindy, who seemed to have no interest in any males. She lived in Bayonne. We were known in the church as 'Cindy B' and 'Cindy D.'

One weekend at the end of the summer, I had been on a successful workout, weight-loss program, and was almost thin (at least for my body) for the first time ever. We had spent a lot of summer days together, but I was always restrained, hiding who I really was, thinking it was demure. That day, I was feeling extra confident. Cindy had asked us to take a ride over to her house. John picked me up, and I decided I was going to laugh and be my loud, fun self with no restraints, whether he liked it or not, and I did just that from the minute he picked me up until he dropped me off home. I was doing cartwheels, back bends, cracking jokes, laughing, and really being me all day. I even ate in front of him. In fact, I ate a lot! Cindy's mom made this delicious barbecue-basted turkey, and I was inhaling it because it was turkey! I can still hear John saying, *"Wow, Mola, you're a real piece of work today,"* with a big questioning grin and repeating it over and over again all day long and on our ride home. Something changed after that day. You would not have noticed, but I did, and so did he. He was still being cautious, but I knew he was feeling it too. I'm pretty sure his mom made it clear to him how I felt because I never hid it, but we never discussed it.

Months later, on a cold near-winter night, John and I went to see a movie alone. It has since become an iconic classic Christmas movie, but at that time, it was a new film. I did not watch it at all because it was the first time John ever touched me in a romantic way. He used to drive his Audi Fox like a maniac over the Outerbridge from Tottenville, Staten Island, to New Jersey so we could go to a better movie theater. I loved the thrill of it! I remember that December night—it was *freezing* cold, and the heat in his car was not exactly promising. I used to sit on my hands to keep them warm, even if I had gloves on. That night, it was remarkably cold and icy, but I was warm inside from the feelings of love and excitement. I always remember the clothes I was wearing on days that were special. That night, it was dark blue branded jeans, a red sweater with all different-colored hearts in a straight row across my chest and white leather, pointy boots. We walked into the theater together and took our seats.

The movie was playing for about ten minutes, and he was leaning forward watching it intensely. I remember peeking at his serious face (even though the movie was a comedy) and thinking, *What the heck is this movie about?* All I thought of was his perfectly shaped nose and his light eyes, and suddenly it happened.

He didn't look at me, he didn't say anything. He just took my hand, locked his fingers in mine, brought it up to his lips, kissed it, and held it there for the rest of the movie. *I did it! I got him! He loves me too, I knew it all along.* We drove home that night holding hands too. We did not say much. I did not want to say the wrong thing and ruin the night. In reality, I couldn't say anything. I was in a puppy love stupor, drunk with warm and gooey feelings of love that I had never really had before. John dropped me off at home, kissed me softly on the lips, mentioned something about the next day, and screeched away.

I waltzed upstairs to the bathroom, holding the hand he held with my other hand, really believing it was on fire. I felt it. Something was wrong with my hand, but in a good way. I had a super power. It really was tingling. I would never wash it again. Oh my GOD!

The next few times we babysat together, we lay on the couch, cuddling. It was all very innocent—*too* innocent for what I wanted. We never made out. We never kissed intimately. Our relationship was a convenience for him that sort of grew out of a friendship, and though I secretly longed for so much more, I was willing to settle for whatever I got. I was sure he would fall madly in love with me. I mean, how could he resist me? I never said no to him. I was willing to go anywhere he wanted and have fun doing whatever he wanted to do. It is true what is said about puppy love. You get these ooey-gooey feelings complete with butterflies and fireworks, and life is just sweet when you have it. But oh, when it ends, all the clichés about broken hearts are just as true.

John and I were together less and less as the school year became more demanding. He was playing basketball and trying to keep up with his senior year studies and social calendar, and I was still the young sophomore that just transferred to school, unnoticed in a sea of students, blending in like a hunter dressed in khakis in the woods.

Valentine's Day came and went for me. I do not remember anything special about it other than the red Valentine's heart of boxed chocolates my dad always got me. I used to gently smash them from the bottom to see if I liked what was inside. If I did, I delighted in every bite as it slid down my throat into my welcoming stomach.

I am not sure how, but I had learned that John received a pink rose from a fellow senior. I guess the fact that people were talking about it was a really bad thing for me. Valentine's Day roses were part of a high school tradition. If you were friends, you sent a white rose. If you were lovers, you sent a red rose. If you wanted to get to know someone and never had the guts before, you sent the pink rose, which meant, "I like you and I want to get to know you better."

This girl was a foreigner to me—blonde and blue-eyed and not from the youth group. She was not even from church! My young mind could not wrap around the whole thing. I wrestled with everything about me that was opposite of her. Why would he respond to that stupid pink rose? Here I was, a sort-of-pretty, chubby, brown-haired, brown-eyed sophomore. I was living right and doing everything to please God and my parents, perfect for a good guy who seemed to have had the same values and goals as me. Why mess this up? *She was a worldy girl who would do whatever she could to get him,* I thought. I did not know at all if that was true, but somehow, thinking like that made me feel better. All I wanted was to be happy with John, to serve God, and to live a good long life together. That just was not going to happen.

John fell in love with her hard and fast, and they were a hot item. The whole youth group knew it, and I was devastated and desperately trying to exercise my faith and love and not get bitter about it. I felt like a loser, and I was embarrassed, but I knew how to shrug it off in public. John's presence in youth group and church faded. They were always together—inseparable from what I heard. I shut my ears and eyes to their relationship and completely removed myself from it all. It was too painful for me. When they were around as a couple, I snuck away. Although I was sad for my personal loss, I was even sadder that he could lose his passion for the things of God so easily and disconnect from a loving church family, especially after all he had seen and learned about God and His goodness.

By now, transition was happening everywhere. Dad remarried. I knew that our lives would change dramatically, and I felt ready for it. The big house was no longer for just us; she was moving in with one of her two sons, and I wanted my father happy. We would be a family, and the big house would be full of life. The whole thing was really good in the midst of my turmoil with John. My mother was moving forward in her life too in Staten Island, focused on her work and her future, and that was a good thing. I spent time with her on weekends and was glad she was moving on as well.

The raw truth about John was that I felt alone again, and I missed him. He was my friend. I started eating more and throwing up more often, and sometimes I just ate and kept it down. Food always comforted me. John married the girl who sent the pink rose, and they are still married with children, from the last I heard. She really did pull him away from youth group and church, and from what I know, God too. I guess the timing of going to New Jersey to complete high school was not so bad after all. Besides, I was with my dad. He would never drop me like that, and he would never turn away from God and the church. I could depend on God, and I could depend on my dad.

*****

School was so different in suburban New Jersey, and I was aware of it every day. I did not really struggle to make friends because I did not want to make any. I mean, I was friendly, and I never had a problem talking to people, so it was okay. My heart was not into school and achieving anymore. I wanted to move on. I did okay academically, and there are some highlights in my mind, like my public speaking class and the redheaded, bearded (probably) Buddhist teacher. Although my teacher wore a prominent wooden idol on his neck every day, he recognized my passion and excellence and always rewarded my speeches with As. He was especially fond of my "speech to interpret," where I read David and Goliath straight out of the New

International Version of 1 Samuel 17 of the Bible with all the gusto of a young stallion galloping in the wind. He was respectful and complimentary and a breath of fresh air in high school. I remember the students' captivated faces and my hopes that they would be drawn a bit closer to the God of deliverance that I knew so well. I remember the locker room and honest discussions about life as a female teenager and gym class in the middle of the day when we needed to worry more about our lipstick and hair than how many laps we could run around the track. I remember the lunch room and how I just wanted to get to the line first or last but definitely not wait on it long for my pretzel or freshly iced cake. Rarely, if ever, did I eat real, nutritious food. My most memorable person at that school was my band teacher. He was so different than others. I played the trumpet, and so did he. I could hold my own, but I was never great, and this teacher had an interest in students like I had never noticed in others before. As I write this, I learned that he is nominated for a Grammy, not just for his amazing ability to teach, but because of his nurturing. I spent my free periods with him chatting about life and church and music (never playing as he always suggested). I had a small crush on a senior (again). No one ever knew it, and I was sure nothing would ever come of it because I was *way* too insecure and shy, and we came from very different worlds. He was Jewish and Jersey, I was Christian and New York—for starters. The differences were vast and wide. He was one of the most gifted musicians I had ever met. Everyone knew him in the high school music circuit—not just in New Jersey, but in the whole country. Anyway, I never got to know him. I just kept my secret crush a secret and enjoyed it.

By midsenior year in high school, I just wanted it to end. I felt really, really out of place. Between the boring Jersey boys and the snobby skinny girls, I was feeling more and more like I had to move forward. I was eating nothing all day unless I had a weak moment at lunch, where I would eat a soft, hot pretzel or a piece of cake in the cafeteria. I liked all the cakes even though I tended to be more of a savory eater than a sweet eater. The cakes were one-layer, baked in a huge square pan in either vanilla or chocolate, and iced in the opposite flavor. They were cut into individual squares and placed on little white paper plates lined up on the stainless steel counters under glass, easy for us to grab. I always searched for a middle piece of cake. They were evenly high, so I got more for my money. I enjoyed every sweet bite. Once in a while in the cafeteria, it was grilled cheese day. Square pillows dripping with cheese were lined up like soldiers on long rectangular pans behind the counter. I would purchase and sneak down one of those delicious grilled cheese pillows, thick with too much yellow American cheese stuffed sloppily between standard-grade white bread. I remember thinking they were just crispy enough on the edges from the smear of margarine that prevented them from sticking to the pan they were baked on. Most students avoided them, but I secretly loved them. Those skinny, snobby, suburbanites had no idea what they were missing out on. The one problem was that the eating and throwing up was starting to make me really sick. I was having terrible pains in my stomach and would often get really weak in the middle of the day, but I never told anyone. My stepmother used to comment about how pale I was. My blood pressure, if and when checked, was really low. It was getting more difficult to eat and really keep it down, but I could handle it. I could hide it, and I could trust God to fix it.

I had let my grades slip to average because all I cared about, all I wanted, was to be full-time with my father in the ministry. I let go of my passion for English and grammar and my junior high school dreams of medicine, straight As, and academic clubs. Being at the church was more important. I felt like my mission was accomplished in high school, but I secretly hated being average. I hated that I was no longer in the National French Honor Society and National Honor Society. I missed the geeks from the chess club in New York, and I missed their challenges. I craved a little friendly academic competition, but I held all those feelings inside because I really believed I had to in order to help people alongside my dad in ministry. I "preached" in school all the time—not in an annoying way. I was always encouraging people, telling students God was for them and not against them. I would tell friends that God did not require that they stop anything but that they give Him a chance to show His goodness to them. "God is the original author of the statement, healthy, wealthy, and wise," I used to say. I remember my English teacher in tenth grade. He was an articulate and command-ing man who taught us to challenge thinking and push beyond. His coaching helped me win two classroom debates and made me want to join the club so badly because I always enjoyed learning and being challenged. Sadly, I often hid my passion for it because I was always afraid I would be made fun of, and I never wanted to be ridiculed for more than I already was, being overweight in a skinny world.

Church was exciting for me. I was involved in the youth group, and I sat on the edge of my seat to hear and understand every word my father preached from the pulpit. His style is so unique. He is articulate but very real, and he preaches with great passion and with knowledge and wisdom that will help you do what you have to in life! This word that he taught me and that he practices daily helped create a habit of speaking and acting in faith and believing that I could have what I prayed for. Guests who came and preached and taught were sometimes equally as exciting. I especially enjoyed when God would use these men and women of God supernaturally for miracles and prophecy and things you do not see every day. Many of these guests would say things to me that encouraged me and sometimes even call me out telling me things God had for me while reassuring me that the hopes and dreams He placed inside me would come to pass. How could they have known what was inside of me? They couldn't. They spoke under influence. I was full of fire for church and the ministry and always ready with expectation to receive. I could recall many names of preachers that came, but one stands out. He was from the Midwest, and he often spoke prophetically. He was a seer. He could look at you and sort of read your mail. He preached an encouraging message of faith, and then he called me out. Smiling and looking, he said, *"There's a healing taking place in your stomach...God is doing exactly what it is you need."* He said a few more things about my stomach, and then he smiled; and I knew he knew about my little struggle with bulimia, and that although it might try to present itself again, the struggle was over. This man said a few more things about my heart and my future—good things—and I received them and believed them.

Going to eat after church, especially at night, is sort of the thing to do for church-going people. We often went with friends en masse to the local diner and talked about how great the service was while we shared disco fries and cheeseburgers. My dad and stepmother did not like to go out to the diner much at all, but if there were special guests in town and they wanted to go out, they would happily oblige them. At that time of my life, if I did go out, I usually didn't eat much. That night, after we were seated and looking at the menu, the guest speaker looked me in the eye and asked, *"What are you going to eat, Cynthia, darling?"* I felt exposed—but in a good way—and I knew he knew I needed to eat. When I ate the fried shrimp basket I ordered, dipped in standard cocktail sauce and a little tartar too, I knew that I would never have a stomach pain again.

Daily life continued with its basic ups and downs. School and youth group and church were all going along well. I had my fair share of teenage activities and life was okay.

I am not sure why it came up around this time in my life, but I distinctly remember my father bringing up George to me. I guess there must have been some talk of the past and the accusations that always followed George. He sat me down at the kitchen table and assured me that I could be honest and that it was okay but that he wanted to know if George had ever tried anything with me or touched me. My father is soft and kind when he should be, and he was as soft and kind as he possibly could be that day, looking me square in the eye. As I've said before, my relationship with my dad is honest and open. It is a friendship and camaraderie as much as it is a father-daughter relationship. I trust him, and he trusts me. So, when he asked me that question and looked me square in the eye, I cannot explain why I looked right at him, shook my head, and vehemently denied it. *"No, Dad! Absolutely not!"*

Lowering his voice and leaning closer, he said, *"Are you sure, honey? Are you sure? You can tell me. It's okay."* I continued to deny it, and he believed me. I do not know why I did not tell my dad, but my guess is a combination of fear and shame and guilt and what a total disappointment I would have been to him. But I was not comfortable with not telling my father the truth. In some way denying made me feel that the horrors of this experience never took place, although I was not happy that I actually protected George. That conversation would replay in mind often, but it was too late to fix at that point.

Overseas crusades were the highlights of my years, and Dad was planning them a lot. Our focus was the Caribbean. It was my opportunity to shine with Dad. I remember a trip to Jamaica. As a young girl, I was in charge of the children's crusade. Ten thousand kids showed up in that park, and I will never forget the feeling on that stage with the bright sun beating down on my exposed neck. Those children pulled everything in me out over a two-week period, which included lots of church and orphanage visits that just broke my heart.

Someone else was on that trip—George. I was still unnecessarily friendly to him and still really confused about my feelings for him. The attention he gave me always felt so good before we got alone. Then I would just feel guilty and dirty. Toward the end of an impactful crusade and missions trip, he followed me to my hotel room. My roommate was out somewhere, and I was scared to death. I knew I could not talk my way out of it. I could try, but I would lose. I was too tired to try and too scared that someone would see him near my room to keep him out. He came in quickly after me and immediately moved close to me, and I remembered how much I hated his tongue. Without warning, he put his hand down my shirt, closed his eyes, and said, *"Mmmm, you smell so good, Chince...sooooo gooood."* I felt ten years old again. It is a memory I will never forget. I felt shame and disgust. I was there to help people. This was a mission's trip! I managed to pull away and send him out, but that part of my life was still not over. I ate some chocolate candy to comfort me and went to sleep to try and forget it. Ministry was my reason for being there, and there was more to be done before we left.

Boarding the plane with the crusade team to head back home for rest and recovery felt good. I was feeling so tired and weak on the flight home. I assumed the fatigue I felt was normal, a result of hard work and emotional ups and downs after ministering so much to so many. I was afraid to eat in Jamaica just because it was not American food and international travel was new. I ate a lot fruit and occasionally some french fries, but not much else. We touched down back in New Jersey, and I went to school the next day with a raging fever and sudden, severe diarrhea. I was sent home by the school nurse and lost twelve pounds in a few days, fighting some sort of gastric upset. But thank God, I recovered fully at home with rest and fluids and the toilet bowl beside me. I recovered with enough time to sink back into the drudgery of the end of high school.

As June rapidly approached, the usual end of high school events ensued. I had a boyfriend as the prom approached. He was from church, and I was enjoying our relationship but had no desire to go to the prom with him and the boring Jersey boys and the snooty Jersey girls. My boyfriend had graduated a few years before, and we were more interested in going to the church formal anniversary dinner. I would get a great dress, and we would share a limo with friends and go out after it. More than a thousand people would be there, along with my family and friends from church, and we planned to have a great time there as the perfect alternative.

Preparing for graduation, my high school yearbook had comments like, *"We will see you on the preaching channel"* and *"Keep preaching, girl!"* I took those sentiments to heart and was proud of my reputation.

Graduation came and went, and off to the ministry I went. Well, not really. I was placed in the accounting office to do clerical work. I saw it as an opportunity to use my head and was excited to be an employee of the ministry. I went to work happily, knowing there were more crusades coming, and I plugged into youth and children's ministry and whatever else I could.

Chapter 9

Whatever Your Hand Finds to Do

Life is about transition; seasons. It is about people, places, and things that come and go in our lives. I am learning that although we do not like to accept the downs of life or the suffering we endure, it is these downs that help us to understand the ups. In fact, these early seasons that are not exactly the height of 'summer vacation' are crucial to recognize as being part of a process. They are often setups for what is coming. Being consistent, speaking and thinking positively, and doing whatever it is we are doing in whatever season of life we are in with a whole heart is just setup for the future. We need to give God the right attitude and a willing heart to work with to get us to a season that is more enjoyable. Whatever we put our hand to, we should do wholeheartedly. This attitude invites all the good God has waiting down the road. Attitude is in the success equation to compensate for anything else lacking in our lives. We do not need a high IQ, or the perfect relationship or to be financially secure. There are surely genius minds in the poorest places all over the world with even poorer attitudes. Attitude will ultimately open doors which otherwise would remain closed.

*****

Working at the church in the accounting office was getting old fast. I remember nearly breaking down to my dad in private begging him to let me go to college. He said it was fine if I took a few classes, so I did. I registered for mostly business classes, thinking I could help with office and church business. I liked being in school again, and I was definitely going for As here. We had an assignment to pick stocks from the market and buy shares and sell when we wanted. I picked a stock during that class, that made about $75,000 in four weeks with a very small initial investment (I do not remember exactly how much). My teacher's reaction is still in my head. He could not believe it. I felt vindicated. I felt good. I wanted more.

As much as I liked business, I wanted to use it for the church, so daddy eventually put me in a position where I could use my head and some creative juices too. The department did not even have a name yet, but I was taught how to use an Apple computer and was introduced to the world of desktop publishing. When I became comfortable and the person who was training me moved on, I was given the privilege of running the no-name department. The lady that worked there and introduced me to desktop publishing programs had started calling it Publications, so that became the official department name. I was responsible for communications within the church and for the church. It was exhilarating. I helped develop it into something special. Well-known preachers with very successful churches and ministries routinely commented to me about our artwork and print work, and I was proud. The everyday workings of the department were fun and challenging. I liked the work and the challenge of building the department and communications, but I was not completely satisfied. The desire to do more and even to pursue my own passions was eating away at me inside, and I would suppress it. I could hide it, and I would even cover it with activities and trips and whatever could keep me busy, but working at the church and not actually doing ministry always left me feeling a little bit unsatisfied.

I began to feel like I should take my competitive nature elsewhere and earn some real respect. These feelings caused me to eat more and more. Food was a comfort in the moment of sadness. It was contentment in fun times and celebrations. When I felt sad and empty, food made me feel temporarily happy and full. Food was my best friend and my worst enemy.

I started feeling trapped and frustrated, and my attitude started coming across as angry and discontented. I spoke to my stepmother about it all. She was supportive and willing to help. She never discouraged being proactive about health.

Her idea was that I take some time to go away and focus on my body image and weight-loss goals to get my head straight. I immediately took her advice. I searched feverishly for fitness camps in exotic locations, and I ended up hiking in the famous red rock of southern Utah for a month.

Daily hiking in Utah in perfect September weather and breathing in what is probably the cleanest air in the United States was challenging and stimulating. I experienced things I would never trade, but the best thing about going there was meeting my still–best friend, Lisa. She walked up to me in a cafeteria with a gorgeous face, big brown brilliant eyes, and long curly, out-of-control locks that were desperately trying to escape the scrunchie on top of her head. In a distinct Cleveland accent, she looked me square in the eye and asked, *"Are you Itaaaalian?"*

I was sitting with a tray of strange, vegan food in front of me. Although it was not recognizable, I could not wait to dig into it because I was starving and worked up an appetite with a very full day of extreme exercise. I looked up at her a little disconcerted, but I welcomed the fact that she noticed I was Italian (no matter how she pronounced it). The second I replied with a *"Yes,"* she sat down beside me and extended a tiny, warm hand with hot-pink-painted nails that matched her shirt.

"Hi, I'm Leeeesah." We were instant friends (not an easy thing for a semireclusive, private, Christian church girl with a weight problem from New York). We spent every moment there together, playing sports, walking, hiking, and working out in the gym. Our days and nights were full of activity. We laughed and talked and walked and sweated and hiked in the early mornings and late afternoons. We sunbathed and shared our likes and differences, relaxing for a few hours every day under a picture-perfect baby-blue sky, in weather

I have never experienced again since. We compared and contrasted every detail of each of our very different yet similar lives. We even rented a car and took weekend trips to see Bryce Canyon and other famous landmarks in different states like Nevada and Southern Arizona, where we saw the Grand Canyon. We always managed to create an adventure that got us into some sort of situation we either laughed our way out of or ran as fast as we could from. We mistakenly drove into a polygamist village on one of our weekend excursions in Utah. It was as remote and freaky as you see on television, and we probably ended up there because we were talking and not paying attention at all. Dirt roads and women with the same long braids dressed in prairie dresses were all we saw. Trailers with multiple doors and straight-faced, country-looking men, some with visible shotguns, and kids running all over the place were all around. I was petrified that I might never see New Jersey again. It was so creepy. Everything was arid and dusty and so dull and old. It was another world for sure—sad and isolated and far removed from modern society. Lisa made me pull over to go into what looked like a department store—the only thing there besides trailers—but it wasn't a real store at all. Lisa was picking through a huge pile of used shoes thrown into a big metal bin with a long stick, making fun. Every eye was on us, and someone was watching a little too close. We got out of there quick. She giggled and laughed, and I hit the gas, never looking back. Only with Lisa!

None of the amazing landscapes we saw or fun trips we took could compare to how well we got along. We had a bond that would be proven through the years. She was the reason I picked Utah. I am sure of that.

In addition to meeting Lisa, I lost about forty pounds and went home feeling like a tanned, fit athlete. I felt rested and recuperated. I had some mental peace—you know the kind of peace that comes after a good vacation; the kind that is passing.

I returned to work happy. My hair was long and a lot lighter from the sun exposure, and my skin was fresh and tan. I put on a much smaller outfit—a very fitted, nontraditional, black suit jacket that zipped up the center. It had a six-inch-wide hot pink vertical stripe down the center and a short black matching skirt. I was no model, but I felt confident and pretty. I felt attractive and sexy. Coworkers and friends were warm and complimentary the first week of my return as I settled back into my life. I continued to exercise and did my best to eat right, but it did not take long for the mental peace to fade. I was working at the church, in a very cool corner office with an assistant and pretty good success but I still felt that there was so much more out there for me. I was happier away from my life. Now I was back to it full swing, struggling to maintain the weight loss and confidence and overall happiness that was already fading.

Chapter 10

Healing

Healing sometimes can be so difficult for us, but it is easy for God. He is the one who made cells so sophisticated that they start repairing simple and deep wounds immediately, microscopically, overnight. For us, it does not really feel easy but if you think about it, we do not really have to do anything but go through the process. We just have to accept it. We just have to believe it. It is a process of realizing that He is good and that love is His nature, so healing is who He is. Sometimes we delay the final outcome of what the process is intended to produce. As I have stated, I have this wonderful, amazing father who makes trusting and loving God easy. Often, how you see your parents is how you see the Father God. I struggled to be whole, struggled to accept that a simple recognition of God's goodness would shine down on all my inner darkness and burn it away. I just had to let it shine. I just had to see it for what it is—good.

Some of the struggle for me was just wishing I could be anyone but me. Why couldn't I be more compromising and less demanding? Why couldn't I relax just a bit more and not always go for broke? Why couldn't I look like Heidi Klum—tall and oh-so-lean with a perfect nose and sexy eyes? Or why couldn't I play the piano effortlessly like Stevie Wonder or run like the wind with the grace and strength of an Olympian? Occasionally, in a weak moment, I will still feel these feelings, but not too often anymore. I am not Heidi

Klum or anyone else. I am me, made by this good God. If I really believe what I live and speak, I am made in the image of God. I am wonderfully made. I was made to be me. I was made for a purpose. It is time to stop fighting it. It is time to accept and embrace it. It is time to love me. It is time to heal. It is time to believe I am who I am because He made me, and what He does is perfect.

*****

Month after month, year after year, project after project, relationship after relationship (without the hope of it becoming permanent), and just plain disappointment led me back again to questioning what I wanted out of life.

Lisa was visiting from Ohio at least twice a year, and every visit was so much fun. Our friendship and our times of adventure together were the highlights of my year, but it just was not enough. Lisa and I shared the weight-loss struggle for many years, so we were always on another diet, trying to meet a new guy. She was loving her life, working as a dispatcher for the Cleveland police, and it did not take long for her to meet someone special. I went to Cleveland to meet him too, and it was so different and so disappointing. I did not like him at all, but more than that, Lisa only cared about what he did and where he was, and we sat in her apartment doing literally nothing but waiting for him for days. I finally had enough and got in my car to drive back to New Jersey, crying my eyes out for six of the eight hours home, knowing I lost one of my best friends in the world and that things with us would change, and our times together, if any, would be few and far between.

My stepmother became aware again of my disillusionment. She suggested that I take a break again, reminding me how well Utah worked for me. I listened, but I did not want to fly, especially across the country. I was too afraid. I found another place that offered diet and fitness and behavior modification therapy. Lisa begged me to go back to Utah; she even said she would go there for a week or so, but I wanted something else, something fresh. There seemed to be many interesting components to a new program that I found. It was in

Hilton Head, South Carolina, and since I was afraid to fly, I would be able to drive there in a day. Besides that, what was appealing to me was that this center not only dealt with weight loss, through fitness and food, there were personal counselors and a psychologist. I spent time researching the available places and decided this was the one. I booked it and was off in less than a month. I arrived to a completely different environment than in Utah. The housing was much more comfortable, the landscape was flat, and the food was gourmet. I traded the hiking for biking, and I did about fifty miles a day as well as swimming, racquetball, trail walks, weights and aerobics.

What is by far the most memorable thing about that trip to Hilton Head was sitting in a behavior-modification class with a small group of successful people, some of whom were there to break other bad habits, like smoking. I could not believe most of them were falling asleep, fidgeting in their seats, and yawning openly in the room. I was sitting in the front row, hanging on to every word, taking notes so intensely, like if I did not memorize every word, I would not live. I was breathing in that stuff like a person who had been suffocated and was just given pure oxygen. I wrote down every single word I could. I loved the speaker's British accent. I loved how he articulated and enunciated. I loved how he emphasized what he was teaching without ever really raising his voice. At the end of that session, I was desperate for more. He told us he was available for private sessions, and I wanted it so bad, but I was petrified to make that known. I wanted a chance to get out everything I had bottled up inside from my childhood. I wanted to know it was okay that I wanted to stop working for the church and pursue something else, but I felt too embarrassed to talk to him. I moved to the back of the room and sat in a seat, pretending to look at my notes. There, I prayed a quiet prayer, out loud, but under my breath.

"Lord, if I am supposed to share things about me with him and if he can help me find my way, let him approach me."

Being raised in a home where we were taught to trust God had me confused about seeking help from someone who did not know all I did about the Bible, faith, and trusting. I do not think it was just about how I was raised. I think my personality and my type A thinking had me always putting pressure on myself that I could work it all out on my own. I did not know if he was a person who trusted God, and that was so important to me. I felt like I was doing something wrong, but I was, in that moment, going with the flow, beyond reason. (My reasoning made no sense anyway.) No one ever told me I could not talk to someone about my life. No one ever told me I could not seek counsel if I needed it. I just acted in the moment, and I am really glad that I did. Still staring down, I was not there for more than a few minutes before I felt the doctor's hand on my shoulder.

"Did you want to talk to me?" he asked warmly, his British accent singing to me.

I could not believe my ears as I felt them get hot and red with a combination of fear and embarrassment. I giggled nervously, feeling that this was clear confirmation to proceed. I scheduled to talk to him the next day. Amazed and excited, I jumped up and headed for the gym.

*****

I continue to think it is funny how I remember the outfits I was wearing on significant days in my life. I know what I was wearing when I experienced true romantic feelings in high school. I know what I was wearing the first time my husband told me he liked my hair. I know what I was wearing many times on first dates throughout my life, and I know what I was wearing the day I treaded lightly into Dr. R.'s office. It was a black lightweight, short-sleeved, hooded sweat suit with matching slip-on sneakers. I was in new territory that day. It was like landing in China and not speaking Chinese, but I was excited for this new language.

The room was warm and inviting. He greeted me with a smile and invited me to sit in one of the two big leather chairs in front of his desk. I chose the one on the right. He sat in the other one. I was so worried about breaking "Christian protocols" and saying the wrong things and not being a good example. I had thoughts about cancelling all night, but it was too late now, and I really was excited.

"So, Cynthiaaaaa, is it?" He looked at me, I nodded. *"What can I do for you today?"*

I opened my mouth to talk, but nothing came out; and like a pot of boiling oil, I began to bubble over. Tears broke out from my eyes like missiles headed to a target, unable to be caught. I could not speak. I could not say a word. I was mortified. I did not expect this to happen, and I was unprepared to handle it. Besides, I was *fine*, wasn't I?! I mean, I had to lose some more weight (what else was new), and I was considering career and college paths, but what was *this*?! What was wrong?

He just kept saying, *"It's okay. It's puuurrrfectly fine,"* but I was a complete mess. No matter how I tried to tell myself inside to GET A GRIP, I could not stop crying. So I stopped fighting it. I cried and cried and cried and cried. I kept raising my hand and my eyebrows to him in apologetic gestures of disbelief. He was really nice and professional about it, gesturing back that it was okay. I did catch him glance at his watch a few times, and at the end of forty-five minutes, I was kind of disappointed that I had to pay a man to watch me cry. But something broke inside of me that day. The floodgates of frustration and fear and disappointment opened from deep inside. It was the beginning of healing for me inside and of acceptance of who I was.

When I went back the next day I was afraid of a repeat episode, but I did feel some relief. I was ready to speak, and by the end of a session of saying what I really thought and felt—no holds barred— the doctor looked at me blankly and said, *"So, you are telling me that you believe God lives in you, but He shares that space with a lot of darkness that you keep there too? The way I see it; that just does not make sense. Light and darkness cannot be together at the same time. Either God lives in you or He doesn't."*

At first, I felt embarrassed. I knew this well. It was even in the Bible! I began to let go of my pride, and the embarrassment slipped away. I remembered that I was there to deal with some hidden things about me and that is was okay, and suddenly, I got it. It was a light-bulb-over-the-head moment. I mean, I *really* got what he said, and he was right. For the first time, I spoke about the first summer with

George and how the molestation started and how he still called me. Dr. R. helped me begin to deal with that. He made me see how inappropriate and how wrong it was. He explained that because George made so light of the molesting and was so funny and made me feel special as a child, I struggled to differentiate bad and good. It would be a long time before I truly confronted and dealt with it, but those sessions were the beginning of true healing for me and the start of real change in my life. I feel very grateful for it.

I spoke to Dr. R. a third time before leaving that place. He helped me come to some decisions. One of which was that I was going back to college, but not like before. I would go back to college as soon as I got home—full-time—in pursuit of a degree. He helped me understand that I would not be abandoning my father by living my life.

I spent the remainder of my time there biking, swimming, walking, and playing racquetball with a girl named Theresa from Long Island. She was a New Yorker, and we laughed a lot about things we could relate to while working hard to shed the pounds. We enjoyed our meals there, especially the dinners. They were much more gourmet than the vegan Utah surprises Lisa and I shared a few years before.

I spoke to my parents on the phone before leaving to drive twelve hours home. They were excited to see me after missing me for a month, and they heard something good in my voice. I told them I had great news and had made some decisions. I spoke about Dr. R. and how great he was and how I spoke to him privately. I waited to tell the big news in person.

I was welcomed home with open arms. I had lost a good amount of weight and was rested and tanned. They told me I looked great and asked about the trip. I shared the silly details of my stay and the program. I gave them a few things I picked up for them during my stay.

Later that day, sitting on the floor in my bedroom next to the window that faced the front yard, My stepmother got straight to the point, as she smiled and asked, *"So, what is the news?"*

I was sitting on my bed (that I missed terribly), and she was looking up at me. She was supportive when I talked about my aspirations, but this was not easy to say. It wasn't just about how I could go to college full-time at an accelerated pace; I was the head of two growing departments at the church, and she was the one who would have to figure out who and how to replace me.

"I made good decisions there. It was amazing," I said. Deep breath. *"The first is, I am going to college."*

"Great!" she said.

And before I could let her say more, I blurted out, *"Full-time."*

Crystal-blue, surprised eyes opened, and an unsure but light-hearted, elongated *"Okayyyy"* came out of her. She got it. When it came to school, she always got it. Immediately she started to plan.

The next few days, we worked out all the details together. I could switch to working part-time at the office and focus on the conference planning I was doing. They would replace me as department head in Publications, and she would talk to dad. I was so afraid of hurting him, and I knew by letting her tell him, it would be a little easier. He, of course, was supportive. I registered full-time, and my dad even drove me to the registrar's office.

I was running the International Pastor's and Minister's Conference for my dad as well as Publications. I took his vision for a minister's conference and ran with it. After many discussions with him and a lot of research I did about advertising and planning and running a great conference in the few years I was over it, it had gone from a small, church-based conference with a couple hundred pastors to a huge, five-thousand-plus people event with over one hundred nations attending and well-known speakers from around the world. We had amazing presentations about the nations and the vision of touching the world with state-of-the-art staging and lighting and publications. It was amazing, but I could not wait for my classes to start, especially Psychology 101, thanks to Dr. R.

I had learned things in the last month at a fitness camp that I had never really learned before, and I had a growing appetite for more. Dr. R spoke of basic psychology concepts that I still remember today. Psychology 101 was among the first classes I took. I took twelve credits the first semester and got As straight across the board. I was the first one in the classrooms and the last to leave. I became president of the Psychology Club, and I mastered most of the academic challenges I was presented with. I even won Rutgers University first-ever psychology research paper writing competition. My paper was on "Type A and B Behavior and Sleep Patterns." I won best in my category and best overall. My award was $150 and a weekend trip to Napa, California. I never took the trip because of my flying phobia, but it did not matter. The trip was irrelevant anyway. I had everything I wanted. I was on the right course.

Chapter 11

That Moment When

There are moments in our lives that are marked. The obvious ones we all know about: graduation, engagement, wedding, the birth of a child, anniversaries. These are not the moments that I am talking about. I am talking about moments in our lives when there is a big, loud, Big Ben bell that goes off in the quiet moment of our thoughts or during some activity. These moments have the potential to transform us. If we pay attention to the stillness inside, instead of the madness around us, the stillness speaks very loudly. These moments do not just occur at special times. They often come at times we need guidance but what we have searched has not helped. Some people call them 'ah-ha moments.' I see them as turning points—flashes of light that help illuminate the path we are walking. Sometimes we have to quiet the outside noise to hear. We have to dim the lights to see. We have to tune in and listen clearly, and we have to follow.

*****

By Psychology 102, I had taken quite a few courses, almost enough to fill a full year of college. I had made straight As and had a perfect grade point average. One of my college friends once advised me, "Do not worry about As, only the credit will transfer when you choose your major." I did not pay much attention to that, mostly because I liked to earn As. Good thing I didn't listen because she was very wrong! My GPA counted for a lot both personally and in my education.

It was just another day of college and I was loving every minute. I loved walking the campus. I loved sitting with an opened book and a pen at the tables and chairs that were scattered all around the inside and outside of the various buildings on the campus. I loved arriving early to go to the snack shop to buy (what else) a pretzel—sometimes a cheese-filled one. Most of all, I loved sitting in my seat, especially in my psychology class, which was held in one of the auditorium classrooms. It was school as usual one day when I was sitting in the Psychology 102 auditorium. I was still the president of the Psych Club and was well liked by Dr. O., the chair of the department, who was teaching this class. We had discussed declaring psychology as my major. I loved what Dr. R. did to help me in South Carolina, and I was always very quick to listen to and help anyone who wanted advice. I felt that I was on the right path, and I loved learning this interesting subject that seemed to touch everyone, every day.

Dr. O. began to teach on the subject of sensation and perception. She was talking about how we all use our senses to hear and see and feel and smell but we all perceive—process and conclude about what we sense—differently. For example, two people can hear a piece of music. One cannot forget it because they enjoy it so much, and the other cannot forget it fast enough. One can eat a certain food and love it and another will hate it. We all sense with the same anatomy and physiology, we have the same equipment, we just interpret the information differently. I was taking copious notes as usual when I looked up to see what was being projected on the board and I saw a large drawing of an eye with labeled anatomy. Immediately, my heart began to pound, and my palms got sweaty. I started to breathe more rapidly, and I could not focus on what was being taught. Everything became a bit blurry, and I had the sensation I might pass out. For a split second, I panicked, thinking something was wrong physically, and then suddenly—*CLICK*—the inside light turned on bright. In that moment, I remembered all the times as a child that I had drawn different parts of our anatomy—the eye, the ear, the heart—on to poster paper for extra credit in elementary and middle school. I remembered how I aspired to practice medicine for so many years but had let that dream fade away slowly, and then suddenly, everything become very clear. I knew what my major was going to be—biology. *I am going to be a doctor,* I thought. *I am going to medical school!*

I barely made it through that class. I was so excited to race home and tell my dad. I finished the full day of school and zipped home as fast as I could much later that afternoon. When I arrived home into early evening, my father was getting ready for church in his room. It was a Thursday. I could hear his shoes, so I knew he was dressed, and I knocked on his bedroom door with excitement racing through me. "*Come in,*" he called out gently. Seeing me, he smiled with his twinkly eyes, tying the knot in his tie. *"Hi, honey, how was your day?"* he asked.

"Amazing! Great day! I know what I am going to do," I said, baiting him.

He was looking in his floor-length mirror, perfecting his knot. *"Mmmhmmm, and what is that?"* he asked, unsure of where I was going.

"I'm going to medical school. I'm gonna be a doctor!" I could not wait for his reaction. I knew he would be happy. He was my rock. He was my always-proud father. Besides, who wouldn't be happy when their child declares something like that?

He looked at me and waved his hand in an 'Oh, you know that's never gonna happen kind of way,' and laughed and said, *"Awwww, get out of here!"*

I know he did not realize how I heard his reaction, and I know he did not mean to hurt me, but my reaction was impulsive, "*No, Dad. I WILL GO TO MEDICAL SCHOOL! You mark my words!"* I raised my voice affirming it, not in a bratty way, but in a confident way as I marched out of his room and into mine. If anyone was going to stop me, it would be me. My heart was pounding. He followed me out, realizing his comment was hurtful and not supportive, so he corrected it immediately.

"Honey, honey, I didn't mean to hurt you. You can do whatever you want to do."

"I can and I will! Oh yes, I will." I said with confidence and a little arrogance. I could taste it now, and I would not be convinced otherwise.

I went to school the next morning much earlier than usual so that I could do some research and get my applications together for medical school. It was an unfamiliar process, but I was good at research and was asking the guidance counselors for help. That week, I hit the career center. It was a special set of rooms that were full of computers with information about various career paths. I researched everything, including the way to pay for the best schools. My siblings made fun of me in a "Here we go again" sort of way about my life change. They never thought I would graduate let alone finish medical school, but I knew where I was headed, and there was no stopping me. I drew from the wisdom of good friends that were older than me who I had met at church, in particular Bob and Linda. Bob was successful in business, and Linda was a physician. They spent most of their free time volunteering at the church and were very active members. I spent time having dinner and hanging out with them. They were fun and smart and committed to God, and they were always so genuine about pouring into my life and the lives of my parents. I attended seminars held in teaching hospitals with Linda, like "How to Become a Medical Doctor." She shared a lot with me about the reality of becoming and being a doctor. I tried desperately to absorb her truths and really be practical about my pursuit of medicine. In all my research, I stumbled upon the job title "physician assistant." I had never heard of it before. I read all I could about it. I even used social media to message strangers around the country who had "PA" or "physician assistant" in their profile to ask about their career because I was so unfamiliar with it. When I learned that I could practice medicine just like a doctor; diagnose, treat, prescribe, and even do procedures, as long as I was with a doctor, I made lists of the pros and cons of being an MD and the pros and cons of being a PA. I chose PA almost immediately because the pros far outweighed the cons, and the opposite seemed to be true of MD. Shortly thereafter, I selected the school. It was in Staten Island—a place all too familiar. My dreams were about to be realized.

Chapter 12

Life Is Difficult

L ife is difficult. I read this once in a best-selling, self-help book, which really did have amazing insight about choosing a path in life that seems to be taken less. I may have even read it twice. It helped me through transition. I committed many of the principles in it to memory and applied them when necessary as much as I could. I remember the author talking about Christianity and how it "made the most sense" after studying world religions because a deity became humanity and could actually feel what we feel. That spoke volumes to me. Christianity is not only something you feel. It is logical. It makes sense. This insight prompted me to embrace certain principles in the book more firmly. I embraced it and preached it all the while learning that we have grown up believing happiness was equal to easy or fair. Somehow as children, we develop this idea that life should be fair and easy to navigate through and if we are good and do right we always get what we want.

"It's not fair!" is screamed quite a lot in schoolyards, homes, and playgrounds when a child feels they have been wronged. Where did this concept of fairness come from? Where did we learn it? Who said life was fair? Fair to one is not necessarily fair to another, and fairness is not a quality that builds character or helps us learn to adjust, so why is it such a pervasive way of thinking? Why does it start when we are so young?

We must be able to alter our thinking and change our plan. We must learn to bend and not break. If a palm tree does not bend in a tropical storm, it will snap and be destroyed and probably destroy everything around it. If there is no give to a rope, the tension will make it break. Things in nature are often created in such a way that they can handle pressure. It is often just a slight movement or adjustment, a matter of simple physics, that preserve things from breaking. I am not talking here about changing and bending to compromise beliefs or lower standards. I am not talking about conforming and giving in. I am talking about being able to adjust, to change just enough to get through a tough situation without breaking. We all know the analogy of fire and purifying gold and of diamonds in the rough. There is something to be said about a fiery process that sometimes takes time and pressure, and the end result is usually amazing.

To live life to its fullest, free from devastating setbacks, enjoying the things most of us want in life, we must be able to adapt. We do our best to prepare and plan and stay on the path to fulfill our destiny. Life will inevitably throw some curveballs. Even the best planning and preparing is not always enough. We must have courage to believe that come what may, we can use the pressure of the experience to allow our true selves to shine through. We can adjust our sails to survive the strong winds of the storm. We can allow the fires of life to refine us and come out purified, not charred. We can reboot the system without losing the precious data we have worked hard to compile and use it not only to get through, but to come out stronger.

*****

I had been working hard toward my goal of being accepted into physician assistant school. I was commuting from New Jersey to New York to go to college while working at the church. I was studying day and night in mostly science courses that usually required a laboratory and an extra day. I studied feverishly, focused on my goal, and successfully completed everything required with honors and in enough time to apply to physician assistant school for the next year. Everything had been working exactly as I had planned (a good thing for a type A personality). I had mapped this all out very carefully and was secretly so proud of my efforts. The next step was applying to physician assistant school. Most people pick two to five schools to apply to and settle for whatever they get. Not me. I had one school selected and one application, which was meticulously printed in black gel-ink pen. All the required documentation was neatly stacked in order in the envelope behind the application. I checked and rechecked everything multiple times on different days for weeks, and then finally, at what I was advised was the right time, I mailed the application with conviction and a strong sense of knowing in my heart, anticipating a favorable reply shortly thereafter.

I waited for weeks, checking the mail almost daily like an obsessed freak. I felt confident that I would be called for an interview, and when the letter finally came, I ripped it open, heart pounding, hands shaking with expectancy. I could barely believe my eyes when I began to read.

"We regret to inform you that you will not be called for interview…" Something was wrong. This was a mistake, wasn't it? It had to be. I had put in so much effort in college. I had worked so hard for this. There had to be a mix-up, some sort of paper error from some secretary in some office who mishandled something. But, it was not a mistake. The bar had been set so high that year that only 4.0 GPAs made the cut, and I was a lowly 3.9. You cannot imagine the disappointment that overtook me. I had come so far, was so driven, so focused, and had done so well that this just did not make sense. I was heartbroken, discouraged. I felt the rug had been pulled out from under me and I was losing my footing completely. Had I worked so hard for nothing? For a fleeting moment, I considered other schools, but it was too late to apply for that year and far too impractical. I shared my letter with my parents, posing with quiet strength, and sobbed deeply into my pillow later in my room. *My siblings were right*, I thought. I would never finish what I started.

*****

The next few weeks were difficult. When you have such high expectancy and you feel so sure, the letdown is really difficult. I received a phone call from Marina, a new friend that I met in college in a biology class who had become a good friend and was on the same professional track as me. Marina had applied with me and had been rejected as well. In her despair, her boyfriend since high school surprised her with an engagement ring and proposal, and she was completely distracted from the rejection of PA school by planning the wedding.

It took a little while before I recognized that this delay of getting into PA school was a temporary setback from reaching my goal, and I would soon see that it was exactly what was supposed to happen to me. I accepted that rejection, let go of it, and decided that I would reapply the following year. My mind was made up about becoming a physician assistant at that particular school, and nothing would stop me. Delay is not denial.

In the next couple of weeks after being rejected from school and getting engaged, Marina was busy planning her wedding. She had decided she could complete everything in enough time to interview and attend the next year of PA school. I thought this was an amazing, hopeful plan and secretly yearned for something to fill my time as well. It was just a few days later that I received a phone call from the head of the biology department of the college I had graduated from.

"Hello, Cynthia! How are you? I am calling to offer you a full-time position teaching anatomy in our lab. We have never really done this before, and you do not yet have the right degree, but in our department meeting, the professors and lab instructors all agreed you are the one. We cannot guarantee you can stay after one year without getting a degree, but we need you now. Are you interested?"

I could not believe my ears! I was going to be paid a good, full-time salary to teach and tutor and study human anatomy. Guess what the very first course was in PA school? Gross human anatomy complete with cadaver dissection. I had ten months to study it and was going to be paid to do so. I do not think I could have planned that more perfectly if I tried. I accepted immediately and called every friend I had to give them the news. Then I headed over to the college to celebrate my new status with my old lab instructor friends.

I spent that year really enjoying my role as anatomy lab instructor, methodically teaching the human body to groups of twenty to forty students and then sitting and tutoring students in an open lab. It was both challenging and rewarding, and the people in the department made it so much fun. Human anatomy gave me a tiny glimpse of what was to come. I learned the material well and enjoyed every moment of it. I was offered the position permanently, and I, for a fleeting moment, considered it. But I knew it was time to reapply to PA school, so I did. Marina reapplied as well. Her wedding was a lot of fun. It was in an amazing three-story hall in Brooklyn that had a lot of character and a lot of marble! I brought one of the lab instructors with me, feeling comfortable with him and his friendship among many of Marina's friends I did not know. It was a great year that was well spent.

Eleven months after starting my teaching at the college, I sat in front of everyone who was anyone in the physician assistant world in New York after being called for an interview. We were told if you got called to interview, you had a more than 90 percent chance of getting in. Although tense, this was my predominant thought as I sat in the waiting room. There were quite a few hopeful PAs-to-be dressed nicely in suits and dresses, waiting in the way-too-hot student lounge. That old building on the North Shore of Staten Island was located very close to the famous Staten Island Ferry Terminal and it had an interesting history and was pretty well-known. I learned in my microbiology class that during the 1940s, tuberculosis research had been conducted there. It was the place for answers, and it brought a good reputation to the old complex for a lot of years. It made me think back to my father being born in the house because of the measles outbreak in the hospitals. The physician assistant program occupied one of the most poorly kept parts of the complex. Everything was old and tired except for the young, eager faces that filled that waiting room. Hearing my name called, I jumped up and made my way in to the tight conference room, dressed in a blue pant suit with a white blouse and shiny blue pointy, patent leather loafers.

Being in the hot seat at a conference table full of medical education directors, physicians with long titles, professors of difficult science subjects, and other who's who in that field was pretty intimidating. I knew that my answers would determine whether my dream of medicine would be realized or not. Question after question was fired at me, and I was starting to feel my sweat drip down the back of my neck like wax melting down a lit candle. I wondered when the questions would stop and when I could get out of there and drink some icy-cold water to cool my hot throat. Although I was feeling it on the inside, I had been holding my own and suddenly felt an unusual calm come over me. I was handling each question with knowledge and grace, watching their faces and feeling good, but now I felt something different—a real confidence. I was asked why I wanted to become a physician assistant and why I chose to pursue this profession. I was even asked what motivated me to do this. I took that opportunity to explain how I was teaching laboratory human anatomy, having been hand selected by the professors in my prior college. Then the last question came from a kind-faced, larger-than-average-sized woman.

"Cynthia, why did you decide to reapply here after not getting in the first time?"

I felt my face get hot and flushed for a fleeting second. I shook myself on the inside, sat up a little taller in my seat, raised my eyebrows, smiled confidently, and let the culmination of everything I had learned until then rise up and flow out of my mouth like a majestic waterfall. "I was sure of my goal. I knew the road I needed to take to get here. The road may have had a few more bends than I expected, but I chose to stay on this path, and here I am." Gesturing with my hand and arm flexed straight out, thumb up, mimicking a straight path, and pushing through, I continued, "It may have taken longer to get here to my goal, and I may have had to alter the route, but I was not going to let anything stop me."

That kind lady with the warm grin was the dean of the Physician Assistant Academic Department for the university. Smiling brightly, she looked around the table at her colleagues with a look and a gesture that I interpreted as "Can we just tell her now?" as she thanked me and told me I was excused and I would hear from the school in a few weeks.

I waited impatiently a second time for notification. This time, I waited with a more realistic expectation; and although I was prepared for another rejection, I had a feeling I was in. It took two weeks, but when I received my acceptance letter, I called Marina immediately. She told me she did not receive hers yet, though she had been interviewed and she thought it went well. I assured her she would get in. It took a few days for her to call me and share her good news. This girl got engaged, married, and was about to enter physician assistant school all in one year. We celebrated together, and I never looked back.

All the planning and studying and preparation for this dream had finally begun to pay off; I was in! Now, it was time to prepare for the next two years of study. We were told that this particular school had a much more intense pace than most. We would begin early each day and end late without a summer break. It was two straight years of work. I did not want to continue the commute from Central Jersey to the North Shore of Staten Island. There would be too much pressure. I lived about fifty-five minutes from the school, and with commuter traffic, early morning tests, late classes, and rotations all around the five boroughs that NYC is comprised of, I was sure I could not live home. Together with my parents, we concluded it was best for me to live close to the school. I was excited to search for a place to live on my own. I searched quite a few locations before stepping my feet into a place that was in a great spot and had so much potential, but it was a disaster and had a disgusting smell. The minute I stepped inside, I knew it was the right place. The damaged, faded mauve carpet was terribly stained with paint (the owner was an artist) and who knows what else. The smell was a mixture of never-cleaned dirt and strong kitchen spices. I knew I would have to redo it, and I was so excited at that prospect. With the help of my parents, I purchased that tiny condo located on the seventh floor of a very cool, safe building. It was priced far below its value because it was in terrible condition, but I was as sure it was my place, as I was alive. I spent a lot of time fixing it up beautifully while taking the prerequisite course of Cadaver

Anatomy. In between studying and preparing for the next two years of intense study, I was at the Home Depot, picking paint and granite and whatever else I could find to make my condominium beautiful. Marina still laughs about us going to the Home Depot daily and how I vacuumed my concrete floors incessantly through the renovations until it was completed. I remember that accomplished and free feeling I had. I was so happy and blessed to have this amazing opportunity. Most physician assistant schools do not have gross human anatomy with cadaver dissection. I reveled in the opportunity to learn that way. I had an amazing instructor, and the people who shared the experience with me made something that should have been so difficult really fun. We learned and laughed and studied together during that hot summer, counting the days for the beginning of the actual full program to start. We were special. We were elite. We had made it this far, and there was no turning back.

After earning an A in gross human anatomy and trying desperately to forget the smell of formaldehyde, I started physician assistant school at what was then St. Vincent Catholic Medical Center, Bayley-Seton Campus. It was a dream come true, for sure. This school held its number three ranking of national PA programs since its beginning in the 1960s. In the first few weeks, elections were held, and Marina and I were voted class co-presidents. I worked very hard and consistently through long days and nights in an extremely accelerated program. I learned so many things in physician assistant school. Most people do not realize that it is medical school—with almost the same amount of study and competition, just not as many years. It is arguably more difficult because medical students take four years to learn what we had to learn in two, and they have summers off and normal breaks in the curriculum. There is a difference in the degree earned and the depth of learning, but we still have to learn every subject in medicine and all about theory and clinical practice. We went straight through two full years. We often had to get up and take tests before school started at six or seven in the morning the first year and then sit in lectures all day until five or six at night, repeating the same the next day in a different subject. I tried to get up three times a week between 4:30 and 5:00 am to walk or run in the park before such a long day. I met so many good people in my class and had a lot of interactions with many, but I became very close to two people in particular—Marina, of course, and Anna. We helped each other through one of the best times of our lives and are still close friends. Anna is a first-generation Italian American from Brooklyn. I loved her immediately. We had an instant connection.

Living on my own and working hard toward graduation was both challenging and amazing. It felt good to be on my own and have the full support of my family. Every so often, I would receive a phone call from George. I remember once talking to him from my apartment. It was IPMC time at church, and I wondered if he was coming. I hung up the phone, disturbed that nothing ever changed with him. He always asked the same inappropriate questions. I thought I had left everything far behind me, but I hadn't. At that time, I do not even know why I spoke with him. As usual, I neither knew how to change this situation, nor if I could. I was dealing with a skilled predator who was sure of his game. He knew how to make me feel ten years old again with fear, shame and guilt. He knew how to call me his 'best buddy' so I would keep my mouth shut. Since writing this, I am sure of what went on then, but at the time I was a lowly pawn on his chessboard. The whole thing was so confusing, so as usual, I opted to just move forward and try to distance myself from it all.

The second year of PA school, doing clinical rotations in different hospitals and medical facilities in the New York metropolitan area was really trying. You are suddenly expected to take all the theory from the classroom and apply it to *real* situations in the hospital on *real* patients at the scrutiny of everyone—doctors, nurses, physician assistants, patients, and patients' families. I cried my way through many frustrations that year. Between the pressure of senior residents and not-so-nice working physician assistants and nurses, I would question myself constantly, all the while wondering what field of medicine I could ever do that I liked enough. Psychiatry was just as crazy as you would think. I literally just missed being on the bad end of a fist that broke a staff member's nose as I breezed past what everyone thought was a catatonic patient. He was not catatonic. He extended a closed fist, hard, directly to the nose of that secretary walking directly behind me.

Medicine on the floors of the hospital was crazy. The pager was non-stop, and the decision making on the floors was very difficult. We were expected to manage many doctor's patients supervised by residents who were overworked and jumped at the chance to temporarily disappear while we were there to cover them. Navigating through the politics was like walking through a minefield. Every so often you would cause an explosion and a nurse, doctor or "mentor" would have a meltdown. If that was an issue, forget about the surgery rotation! I was so sure that the operating room was all I wanted, but after working with surgical nurses that had the personality of Hitler, tired surgeons with huge egos and little respect for physician assistants and even less respect for physician assistant students, I started to wonder why I was even there. The early morning hours, the super-dry skin from scrubbing in, standing in one position for hours while holding still, as well as treating the postoperative patients with horrible infections, was nothing that I thought it would be. I did manage to have an incredible rotation in pediatrics in Brooklyn and Staten Island. I really admired Dr. D., the Italian American pediatrician who ate fresh mozzarella standing up in the break room for a ten-minute lunch while seeing rooms full of infants to seventeen-year-olds all day long. I learned the field well and spent more than double the time I was expected to there, thinking I could do that and do it well until I learned about "well visits." I kept this as a possibility, but I was not completely convinced.

Toward the end of the year, after many doubts on my career choice began to really surface, I did my emergency department rotation. I could finally see the light at the end of a long, dark tunnel: emergency medicine. I could do this. In fact, I liked it so much I stayed longer hours than required, especially with doctors that appreciated my zeal. I tried to put in as many tubes, lines, and sutures as I possibly could. I diagnosed infections and rashes. I stabilized sprains, reduced fractures, and wrapped muscle strains. This is what I wanted. This seemed to be what I hoped for. I was finally relieved and feeling confident of my choices and of my next move.

Two years of excitement, torture and now bliss came as I dressed in my new clothes for graduation. I couldn't wait for the procession to begin. It was as amazing as we hoped it would be. The ceremony was so well done and I felt humbled and proud to celebrate with my class and my family. This wonderful experience marked both the end and beginning of significant chapters of my life.

*****

After graduation, studying was not over. I graduated with high honors, but now, the real pressure was on. I had to pass my boards to become certified to practice medicine. For the next three months, Anna, Marina, and I along with some other graduates met and studied weekly. We would meet in Anna's house in Bensonhurst, Brooklyn, usually sitting around the kitchen table laughing, crying, and eating our way through intense reviews of cardiology, pulmonology, surgery, psychiatry, infectious disease, gastroenterology, pediatrics, and about ten other fields of medicine. We would review *What to Order When* and *How to Interpret ECGs* while devouring Italian mozzarella so fresh it would melt in your hand if it wasn't so sweetly wrapped with prosciutto so thin you could see through it. We would wash that down with bakery bread or melt-in-your-mouth pizza—homemade on the spot by Anna's mother or picked up from the famous L&B's Pizzeria, which was just around the corner. Anna's mother, Theresa, was always there making sure our glasses and bellies were full. She was a welcomed and important part of our study group. Over the next few months, everyone in our group passed the dreaded boards and became certified to practice medicine. I felt proud after receiving confirmation that I passed the boards. We had all worked very hard and worried equally that we would fail but thankfully we all passed. Now it was time to begin the application process to work as a certified physician assistant. I could hardly believe it. What seemed like an impossible thing so many years ago was now a reality. Anxious to take the next step back in New Jersey, I sold my condo after living there for two years for three times what we paid for it. This financial blessing was just another confirmation of my well-ordered steps and

God's timing. I thought I would never want to move back home, but I could not wait to be back in my bed at my daddy's house. It is funny how, as we grow up, we cannot wait to be independent and leave the nest. During rough patches at school, I longed to be in the safety and comfort of my parent's house. The two years of intense pressure and study had made me ready to go home again for good, so I did. There is no feeling of comfort and safety like being at Dad's house. My quality of sleep was so much better.

It was August, two months after graduation and one month after passing the boards. I had been contemplating a strategy on how to approach the physician assistant job market. I was never one to settle for less than I wanted, and I was sure I only wanted to work in an emergency department. Seeing no offers in the places online and papers I checked, I decided to fax my curriculum vitae to three local hospitals. I called each of the emergency rooms there, asking for the fax number and the name of the head of the department. I hoped, sent the faxes, and continued to reason and strategize. I would continue to send faxes to hospitals until I received a call because I was not willing to settle for just any available job.

When I received the call to interview at a hospital that was well known for its emergency services, I had a good feeling that I would be hired. I showed up for the interview as the eighth person to go through the extensive process, which lasted about two weeks. This process had me following around different doctors and nurse practitioners who would test me randomly with questions and give me procedures to do without warning. Although I was the eighth to go through the process, I was the first one offered a position, which I readily accepted. My career path was on fire. I felt accomplished and proud. I beat a lot of odds. I proved my siblings wrong and my instincts right. Now, it was time for love. Life was good.

I was holding my own in one of the busiest ERs in New Jersey and happy doing it. I was working my way through obstacles which came in the form of angry nurses, lazy doctors, cranky nurse practitioners, and challenging patients, but it was what I wanted. In my spare time, I really enjoyed cooking and having people over. People have said it is a talent, my cooking, but I say it is just a really easy and satisfying pleasure in my life. It is a hobby to make good, pretty food, and it is very therapeutic. I have always been able to make great food. I can eat most anything, even something new and unique that I have never had before, differentiate the flavors, and copy it in my own kitchen. I make amazing Italian specialties, but I am really good at other ethnic foods as well. The new modern-American-style cooking is something I could probably do in my sleep. I can even whip up a gourmet meal for a table full of guests in about an hour. It comes naturally, but more than that, it is a relaxing thing that I really enjoy.

One night, my parents had some good friends over. I volunteered to make homemade strombolis, pizzas, calzones, and a fresh salad. I was working on a broccoli rabe and fresh mozzarella stromboli while they ferociously devoured one of the first margarita pizzas I prepared. I remember it so clearly. They were laughing and eating, and George's name came up. He was pastoring in New England in a successful church. I had never told anyone about what I went through since my sessions with Dr. R. in Hilton Head. I was in a very different place in life and in my mind and heart. I felt accomplished. I felt valuable. I felt like if I spoke, people would listen for the first time. I mean, I had run an international conference and had to deal with international pastors, city union carpenters, laborers and stagehands, and I held my own doing that, but where I was now in life was different. It was no longer about my father; it was about me and I secretly reveled in it. My parents and their friends began to lightly jest about the "rumors" about George all those years ago. They were joking about how everything in the old church was such drama. It hit me like a bolt of lightning—caught me dead in my tracks. I felt hot, dizzy, numb. I felt like everything around me was shaking, and then, I just felt angry; pure, red-hot, untethered anger. How could I be so stupid and protect this monster? How long could I keep this in and allow my father to believe he was a good guy? How could I permit this lying, cheating pedophile to get away with this? How much longer would I let him have this power over me?

At the first chance, I cried, I called my sister and brought up his name. Deep down, I always knew he did these things to her too, but she was older than me, and I feared it could have been even worse. We never discussed it before, so I treaded lightly at first; but her nonchalant yet direct, reflex-like responses proved she endured what I did and more. He had gotten to her, and she mentioned my older cousin too. I shivered to think of how many others he had messed with back then and throughout the years. A leopard cannot change his spots. My grandfather quoted this straight from the book of Jeremiah for many years, and I was beginning to understand it.

ENOUGH SILENCE was my only thought after I hung up the phone. I could not even begin to think about how and when I would be brave enough to expose it.

Months later, on a cold, icy early evening for a reason I cannot recall, my stepmother picked me up after a long day of work. This was a unique occurrence. I do not remember whether my car was being serviced or whether my parents did not want me to brave the elements and drive to work alone in my car. It was rare that I did not drive myself anywhere. I remember her picking me up and taking me straight to the nearby drive-through at the bank to deposit my check. We were waiting in a line of cars together, chatting about nonsense. It was a bitter cold day, and there was a lot of snow on the ground. I felt flushed from the heat in the car but my fingers and toes were cold. There was a moment of silence in the car, and there while waiting in the line at the bank, my deep, dark secret crept into the forefront of my mind. Without really thinking it through, I looked at her and told her I needed to tell her something very important. She looked in my eyes, and I began to speak of the horrors of my child-hood experience with George that began when I was just ten years of age. It was as if time stopped and the car began to spin. She was hor-rified, devastated, unable to blink. I will never forget that moment in time—NEVER. I had endured much and I kept it a secret so long. Her blue eyes grew so big they looked like saucers, but the look on her face is indescribable. Shock, disgust, horror, sadness, empathy, love, and anger all rolled up in one face in one moment. I see it in my mind's eye when I think of it, and as many adjectives as I can think of still cannot show you the picture of her face and the feelings it displayed for her and evoked in me. That look was utter healing for me. I do not think she will ever really understand what that reaction did to kill this nightmare—to stop it dead in its tracks for me and to bring me away from it all. It was truly transformational. I know that does not sound possible, but you did not see her face and feel her unbridled passion. That moment is forever sealed in my memory After hugging and crying and sharing a bit, I asked her not to tell my father. At first, she questioned this, but almost immediately she withdrew, respecting my thoughts and feelings. I owed my father the truth, but I just did not feel ready. We drove home with a new bond, and though later we all shared a good family meal as usual, this new revelation shared made everything anything but "usual."

Work was good, though stressful, in the emergency department, and I was considering buying a new place of my own as I settled into my new professional life. The George issue was on my mind, and I wanted time to be able to look my father in the eye and let him know the truth. When the right opportunity came, several months later, I took it. I sat my father down in our kitchen and bravely told him some of what happened to me. George's ministry license expired and was not renewed. He was removed from any ministry connections. I told Jodi that I told them both, and she sat down and wrote him and his wife a very direct letter, explaining that she was free and that his actions had no hold on her. I never felt like writing him, or talking to him or anything like that. I guess God knew I would write it all down for the world to see, and I am sure God knew it would bring healing and complete closure for me and Jodi and for a whole lot of others who need it.

Chapter 13

Bad Decisions Don't Make You Bad

He loved me so good last night. He loved me so good yesterday. He loves me so good all the time. I waited a long time to be loved like this. I waited and wondered and waited and wondered for this—the *real* thing, not the cheap imitation. Heaven. Bliss. What did I do to deserve this?? I am married to the best man on earth—really. He's mine, and he loves imperfect me as if I were perfect.

*****

I was reflecting about a long time ago when a very happy, newly married couple came to our house to stay. They were invited to preach and were staying in our home with us, which was a rare thing. I liked them. They were happy and attractive, and they paid attention to me, so I paid attention to them—close attention. We had just moved into our really nice home in suburban New Jersey. It came complete with four bedrooms, a "bonus" family room, a built-in pool, two garages, and a big backyard. I never thought we would live in a beautiful place like that. I was a teenager and my room was being wall papered. The couple was apt to help, so we went to work on my room. They were so full of life and love and each other, laughing and flirting and enjoying every second of every day. It felt like when you bite your favorite food and your stomach feels it and your mind senses it—ahhhhh—like sitting in a warm, scented bath. I loved seeing and feeling their love, and I knew that was what I wanted too.

In the middle of the day, after lunch, I walked back into my room, looked up at what used to be a bare wall, and saw a lover's heart painted in a dark color with "Debby loves Wyatt forever" in it. You know, the kind of thing girls draw all day in class instead of paying attention, the lover's heart that you always want your name to be written in next to the name of the best guy in your class.

"I hope I can have what you have some day," I blurted out.

Debby immediately came next to me, gently touched my shoulder, and said, *"You can and you will. Say what you want. Say it every day. Believe it. You will have it."*

So I did. I started that night.

"Father, I thank You that my husband loves me like Christ loves His church. I thank You that he is faithful and true to me. I thank You that he loves You first, me second, and my father after me. I thank You that he has a heart after You and after me. I thank You that You are making him everything he needs to be for me and me for him."

I believed it, and I said it every day, with earnest and hope and faith for more than twenty years, missing very few days saying it (if any). And then I met Juliàn, and I stopped saying it. I was sure I did not have to say it anymore. I was sure, he was all I had hoped and believed for.

*****

There are a million clichés, like *"It is not how you start, it is how you finish,"* and *"If one door closes, another will open,"* and I believe them, and they have an important role in encouraging us to get through disappointment. How we reflect on things, how we think about ourselves because of the things we have done, is a lot more crucial than finding another way to get where we want to go. What I mean is if you cannot go back, realize your mistake, acknowledge it, and release it; you really cannot go forward. Sometimes we look back and we feel shame and we feel disappointment, and we feel everything we experienced at that moment we went through it, and the bad feelings and the power of the situation come back. We need to be able to look back at our mistakes, or even our less-than-perfect experiences without allowing those feelings to interfere with where we are now and where we are headed. We need to stop punishing ourselves. We need to release what has already been done. Bad decisions do not make people bad; they are just bad decisions. Sometimes we suffer consequences, but grace can always bring us back. We must let go. We must learn from them and move forward so that all the clichés about success become reality.

Most people have made a lot of poor decisions throughout their lives. After all, we have to make many decisions every single day and some of them are just plain bad. I used to think if we get good guidance and pray hard and trust harder, we would not mess up, at least not enough to matter. Life and love and loss eventually fixed that wrong thinking.

*****

Our first meeting was not special. It wasn't spectacular. I had stopped working as a certified physician assistant in the ER and had been working in nephrology in New York and New Jersey and had gotten really good. In fact, so good my name was known in the area. I had a full-time job and two part-time jobs and a fairly consistent stream of phone calls from doctors, asking if I had time to help them as well.

I walked into this particular clinic late in the afternoon to see the third shift hemodialysis patients. Making patient rounds in various clinics occupied a significant portion of my daily routine. Although my professional life was thriving, I was pretty down on me. I was sure it was too late for me to meet someone special (though I still prayed for it); sure, I was too old. Sure, I was too fat. I was sure I was too screwed up in my head to meet anyone other than a boring old guy

99

with a fetish for a chubby girl—no! My friends were all married with kids, so I made younger friends, secretly hoping to meet *him*.

He had an accent—definitely Spanish, but I was not sure from where, which made it more exciting. I always wanted something exotic. He had a twinkle in his eye and a crooked smile that could make you forget every rule you ever followed and full lips that teased you to kiss them if you dared—and ohhh, if you dared! There was no way. He would not even notice me, but it was always nice to dream.

Coming out of my momentary stupor, I asked someone who he was because I had walked into that place hundreds of times before, never having seen him until then. Eye candy for sure. Big broad shoulders and olive-colored thick arms that your body craved to be held by...

"Him? Oh, that's Julián, the new biomed tech...," and she said it soooo loud. And she giggled, probably thinking he could never be attracted to me. *Shhh! Shut up!* I thought. *Someone will hear that I'm asking!*

And someone did. He heard his name and he saw my face, and he started moving toward me in a sexy stride that he didn't know was sexy. Walking toward me, he smiled a shy smile that made you like him a whole lot more because he looked so good but seemed not to know it, and he asked, *"Can I help you?"*

Intrigued by what I saw and smelled and felt, I could not believe what came out. What was a "biomed" anyway? I was in these clinics all the time, but I never noticed.

Lost in my thoughts and somewhat intoxicated, I blurted out, *"Nice arms. I could use a hug."* Yep, that is what I said. I guess I needed that hug more than I knew because it was the only thing that mattered at that moment. Or maybe it was instinct. Maybe I knew he would do what I asked. He smiled at me again with a little more confidence—just enough—and he opened his welcoming arms wide, jesting easily with a twinkle in his eye and a lateral lisp, you know the kind of lisp that doesn't sound stupid, it just sounds sexy.

"A hug? Ohhhhhh, okay...hahahahaha, 'das easy."

Chapter 14

No One Ever Plans to Fail

No one ever plans to fail. No one ever plans to mess up. No one grows up thinking, *I'm going to dream big but never realize any of my dreams.* We dream, hope, and aspire. We go through life as kids easily saying, *"I'm gonna be a doctor, a teacher, a fireman, an actress,"* in response to the familiar question of what we want to be when we grow up. We never think it won't happen. That is not even an option.

As children, we feel invincible. We dream easily, and we believe they will come true. As we grow up and life happens, the dreams struggle to stay alive, and the pressures of life slowly crush them like flowers walked on in an open field. Every day, those flowers get a little flatter, appearing to have less and less life in them. Most times, the flowers die; but sometimes, they just go to sleep for a long season.

*****

"If you could only understand how much I love you! You just don't really understand...Maybe if you have your own child one day, you will, but I don't know."

"I UNDERSTAND, Dad, and I love you too."

If I could count how many times I have heard this over many years and be paid just dimes for it, I would be so rich! My father's love has been an unrelenting stream of strength and kindness and warmth. It bubbles over like Coca-Cola poured too fast in a tall glass, and it has gotten stronger with time. God forbid I feel any pain! Oh, do I feel sorry for the perpetrator! His love is constant and consistent. It is forceful and honest. It is deep—layers deep and oceans wide. It is gentle but firm. It is divine, and that is why it is so special. If I ever tried to resist it, it followed me like a hungry puppy to an open butcher shop.

My father's love is a wonderful human template of the love of God. It is the reason I can accept and receive the love of God. Father God is gracious and giving and forgiving, like my earthly father, only so much bigger and better because He is perfect. After all, God *is* love. This love my father has covered me with oozes out from his pores. It is rare on earth, but it exists. It is why I am me. It is why I can now receive the same kind of love from my precious husband, but it wasn't always this easy. Maybe it was because of that horrible childhood invasion by a man and the body issues that followed. It could have been the years I spent believing the lies we hear far too often about all our flaws and failures that blinded me to this love. At one time, I struggled to understand why I pursued love that did not look and feel much like what I have just described at all. I mean on the surface, it was warm and kind and gave all the ooey-gooey good feelings; but if you delved just a little deeper, it was just a cheap imitation of the real thing.

*****

I walked to the back of the clinic, my heart pounding. I'm not sure how I knew, but I knew he was back there. I pretended I needed water. He didn't know I usually carried my own. It was a perfectly good excuse. He was sitting at his desk. I saw him turn to me, and I pretended I didn't see him. He stood up fast.

"Helloooo. How are you?" He flashed me an off-balanced, nervous smile. *"You know wha'? I was t'inking I gonna teach you to dance Ba-cha-ta. You know bachata? I's Dominican, like me."*

Before I could answer, I heard footsteps behind me and another Spanish accent. It was a Puerto Rican technician I knew well and liked a lot. She had fire in her walk and a commanding voice and apparently, really good timing. She would help me here. I could not dance, and I did not want to. I called out to her.

"Ophelia? Hey! Guess what? Juliàn is gonna take us out to teach us bachata!"

I was sure he didn't want to take me out anyway. I made it easy for him. A group thing is a good plan. Then I could not show up. I could ditch.

"Oh yeah?" she asked. *"I know how to bachata! Let's go, chica! Tell me when. I'm there!"*

With that, she was out. She marched back to the front to work, and we were alone again. Juliàn acted like that never happened.

"Can I kiss you?" It was the second day I was with him. I felt like butterflies were trapped inside my gut. How could I let them out? They were really starting to hurt. Was I an adult professional? I should not feel this way, and I definitely should not act this way. I am at work! *Get a grip, Cyn. Get a grip!*

"What, here?" We were standing toe to toe in the back of the clinic. My hair was curly. I wished I had blown it straight. I remember the mostly red multicolored shirt I had on. I wished it was black, like I usually wore. Oh, none of that mattered! I was a professional— one step less than the very top of the food chain there. I had to be careful. I was the example, in control. In a second, before I could answer, his hands were gently on my hips and his big soft lips were on mine. I melted. I lost control. *Pleeease, God don't let this end! Please, please, please.* It was so warm, soft, and flavorful. I did not know what I was doing, but I was sure that I never wanted it end.

"You want to go for a ride?" he said softy in his thick accent. Flushed and breathless, I shook my head up and down, and we made our way out the parking lot—separately. We met at my car and got in quickly so no one would see.

"So, what is a biomed, anyway?"

"Oh, we take care of the clinic, you know. We are responsible for maintaining the dialysis machines, the water system, and pretty much the building, you know. I's a lot of work, but i's good."

"Oh, okay. Good to know."

"You know, when I tol' you I want to teach you ba-cha-ta, I meant me and you—alone. Okay?"

There was silence for a minute. Then he turned his head and smiled a boyish smile before he looked down and continued, *"Anyway, I'm sorry for you to see me this way."* He put his hand on his face and drew my attention to what looked like his two- or three-day-old scruff of a beard, as if I cared, as if it didn't make him more exotic and sexy.

"Really? Well I didn't want you to see me like this." I nervously touched my stomach, then my thighs, and then all the "forbidden" parts on me that men usually scoffed at.

Without hesitation, he shook his head and said with emphasis, *"I don't care 'bout dat. I don't care at all 'bout dat. I care about you."* And he kissed me again, slower and softer. I am not sure I had ever felt that way before, but I was sure of one thing at that moment—that I was his completely.

Chapter 15

Facing the Truth

I guess it is all the terrible things we have experienced in life as children that cause us to make poor choices, especially in relationships. Or maybe it is just that what we know to be right is often obscured by what we hope to see and what we want to feel. And in turn, we miss the flashing yellow or blaring red lights directly in front of us. We zoom through these signals, throwing caution to the wind; and with eyes tightly shut, we hit the gas full speed ahead.

I am not really talking about when we are hoping and praying for good results and just sort of coasting and trusting for the right path to be illuminated because that is a good thing. What I am referring to is more along the lines of when your friend asks to borrow money and you hear your dad's voice inside your head, teaching you that it is a really bad idea to mix money with friendships or business with pleasure. The problem is that you are looking the friend in the eye and they are swearing they will pay you back with interest, but you know if you do it, you will be out of your hard-earned dough and eventually out of a good friend too. Still, we usually choose to give the money for fear of the consequences of confrontation, even though innately, we know it is a mistake we will pay for. We just do not have the strength to say no.

Maybe a better example is that terrible feeling you get when you shake the hand of your best friend's new boyfriend and you just cannot make sense of it. He is handsome and so nice and everyone is stoked about him and how happy your friend is to be with him, but you just want to vomit frogs because you have such a bad gut reaction about him. Somehow you know she is (at the least) going to get hurt, but you do nothing because there is nothing for you to do. And eventually, you watch what you sensed unfold in horror.

The question is, why do we ignore signs and regret our actions later? There are no perfect answers, and there is no way to always make the right choices while managing the complexities of life. Although we cannot tell the future, if we learn lessons from past experiences and pay attention to the still small voice inside, we will be able to better predict outcomes and avoid the dangers ahead.

Most of us are trying desperately to be happy, to keep the good friends we have, to compensate for bad decisions of the past, and to meet new people while enjoying good experiences. We want to fall in love, earn a good living, and follow the right path for our lives to have good success. We often decide to pursue a course that is below par, and we suffer the consequences. Although we may grow from a hard lesson learned, the lesson probably could have come at a much cheaper cost.

*****

It had been a few weeks of seeing Juliàn every day. He was very gentle, soft-spoken, and kind. He was sweet, and I enjoyed the hugs, kisses and gentle touches of affection.

I approached him sitting as his desk in the back of the clinic. Smiling widely, he stood up.

"Hellooooo! How are you? So nice to see you." Still smiling wide, but with a boyish grin, he continued. *"I want you to know something,"* he said with a smile that had become uneasy. My stomach dropped, and before I could begin to imagine the possibilities of what was to come next, he blurted out, *"I have someone else."*

Although I could feel my stomach drop to my feet, I was really good at rejection. Like a major league third baseman, catching a would-be line drive, I caught the ball, shook myself on the inside, and threw it to home plate just in time to make a second out. I told him what I had been thinking since we met. Nodding my head up and down and almost snapping my fingers in an "I got this" gesture, I responded quickly, *"That's cool. No problem! This is just about fun anyway, right? This is about dancing ba-cha-ta late at night and an occasional lunch. No relationship, no strings, just fun, fun, fun!"* I smiled and did my best girl-is-in-charge bottom shake and turned to walk away. (I am sure it wasn't pretty.)

Shaking his head with a now-serious face, Juliàn followed me, grabbed my shoulder lightly, and turned me to him. *"No! Nooooo! Naaaa fo' me! You na' yus' fun fo' me! I like you. A LOT. I yus' need some time. I don' love her. I got a little trapped wit' her. I want a RELATIONSHIP with you. Yus' give me a little time. Trus' me."*

"Look, Juliàn. We are from different worlds. We want different things. I am sure I am older than you. It is okay. I understand your situation, and I am flattered that you like me. Let's just have fun. It's cool." I said that, but I did not really mean it. I was already hooked on him, and I knew I could give him time. In my mind, he ticked a lot of the boxes on the secret list all girls write as they go through school. He was exotic, tall, dark, handsome, gentle, hard-working, confident, athletic, and I knew there was more. Besides, I had a secret weapon, something sure to push him away because I was sure I could not push him away on my own.

"Juliàn, I am a committed Christian. I do not want a relationship with someone who does not love Jesus and is in another relationship. Don't worry. It is okay. I am okay." I was sure he would run.

"Wha'? I love Jesus too. I LOVE Jesus!" he near screamed with excitement as he pulled a gold cross out from inside of his shirt and kissed it while standing. His eyes twinkled, and his smile broadened. *"I love Him. I pray a lot. He is everything."*

I should have run. I should have given him an ultimatum. I should have drawn on the experiences of every other woman who ever dealt with this. I should have followed the advice I gave to so many other people so freely. I should have thought of *her*. But I did not move. I did not give him an ultimatum. I did not turn around, go back to the patients, and finish my work. I stayed right there, smiling back at him, swallowing every word he said. He placed both hands on my shoulders and looked into my eyes. I stared straight at him fixated, for fear that he would come to his senses and lose interest in me. *"I don't want to jus' have fun wit' you. I want a relationship. I don' love her. I don' even really like her. I will explain to you. I's a long story. Believe me...I yus' need time."*

He looked so sincere and stared directly into my shy brown eyes; I surrendered. It was not a big deal. We would get to know each other. I would give him time. What could it hurt? It was just lunch. Just ba-cha-ta. He does not love her. He just said that so easily and he made it so clear. He said it more than once without hesitation. It had to be true. What they had was not secure at all. He needed time to end it and then commit to me. We had a connection. I felt it.

We got in my car and talked about what we wanted for lunch. We decided on subs, headed for the deli; and after the first perfect bite of delicious sliced ham, turkey, and mozzarella cheese topped with shredded lettuce, tomato, onion, oregano, sweet peppers, oil, vinegar and mayonnaise, everything was all better.

Chapter 16

Overachiever

"*You are an overachiever.*" I do not remember the first time I heard that, but I know that whenever I do, I feel as though I am being scolded. Aren't you supposed to get As in school? When you do a project, shouldn't it be your goal to be the best? For me, trying to be the best at everything—going for the gusto—made me lose focus and follow a course I knew I should not traverse.

I believed he loved me, and I believed it was simply a matter of time before he left her. I thought she was an obstacle to overcome. I could make him forget her. This was meant to be. I could do anything I wanted to. But as much as I say I could do anything and as much as I really believed it, I could not. There are things we cannot control. Sometimes even if you study really hard and even if you completely learn what you studied, you still get a B.

*****

Our relationship was still pretty polite and formal. Juliàn had invited me to his apartment. It was far from where I lived and on the third floor in an old house in a town with sort of a reputation that I did not know at all and I was really uncomfortable at even the thought of going there. Besides, I did not really know him, and I had never gone to a man's house on my own, especially alone. I was really good at making excuses, but he started to realize that I was uncomfortable.

"I'm shy—REEEALLY shy about it. That's all," I tried to explain.

"Is okay. I understand. We will figure it out." And he flashed that amazing smile of his, and it was okay.

I was seeing him a few times a week and enjoying every exciting moment. He really liked me, at least he made me feel that way. He made me feel special. I welcomed those feelings. They were a long time coming.

I had a friend, Sandy, a Jewish/Italian American girl who loved Latinos and salsa dancing. She was crazy for it all. She roped me into a salsa dancing class once, and I sat in the corner talking to the other suckers like me that were there just to be good friends. I drank iced tea, stared at my watch, and counted the minutes until I could be in the comfort of my bed. When Sandy heard about Juliàn, she assumed he had friends, and she came up with a plan. I was never comfortable going to nightclubs. It was not my nature at all. I always blamed it on the fact that I was fat, but I am also pretty private and I do not like people in my personal space. Beautiful, perfect-bodied people go to clubs to meet people. I was not one of them, but I would do anything to be with him, especially in public! He was so handsome. I wanted him to hold me proudly and openly to prove I could be with a hottie. So, we planned to meet at a trendy, small, Latino club late on a Friday night to dance ba-cha-ta.

Sandy and I had been waiting in the club for about an hour. It was eleven thirty, and they were coming at any moment. I was enjoying the DJ and feeling more excited as the minutes passed and the dressed-up, liquored-up Latinos poured in. I could not wait for her to see how beautiful he was, and he was all mine—well, he would be, soon. We scanned the place looking for attractive guys, amidst a sea of bronze-skinned, bubble-butted, skinny-waisted, salsa-dancing chicas.

I was sitting on a high stool wearing a chocolate-brown, velvet, scoop-necked shirt when I felt the back of her hand slap my chest. *"OH MY GOD...look! Is that HIM?"*

Strutting confidently through the door in a cool, fitted, charcoal-gray sweater, with a freshly shaved face, perfectly gelled hair, and a sexy smirk across his face, towering a full head above the thickening crowd, was Juliàn. His friend, a foot shorter with bulging muscles and a way-too-tight tee shirt, followed him with a smile.

"Oh my God, he is beautiful. Ohhhh myyyy Goooood," she said slowly and exaggerated. Looking next at Ian, she spoke in a more normal tone, *"Hmmm…His friend is behind him, right? Cute. He is okay—not really my type, but okay, he's cute."*

My heart was racing. When our eyes met across the room, I thought it would beat out of my chest. He came right up to me. *"Helloooo baby."* I felt flushed, excited. I bravely leaned in to kiss him, but he did not kiss me. I was not sure how to interpret that, but my self-doubting nature immediately made it about me. I looked bad, I thought. *"This is Ian, mi compadre. He's like my brother. We do everything together."*

I liked Ian immediately. He had kind eyes and an easygoing look on his face. He laughed easily, and you could just tell he was all fun and no drama. Ian liked me too. He kissed me hello on the cheek, chatted with me a bit, and then at Juliàn's prompting, he and Sandy started dancing. I sat back down quick. Juliàn stood in front of me. *"So, how are you, baby?"* His crooked smile broadened, revealing his straight, white teeth.

"I'm good, thank you." Nearly gasping, I continued, *"You look amazing! Wow!"*

"Oh…Hahaha…T'ank you, t'ank you. Dis' how I wanted you to see me…Not like you did at work."

The conversation was sweet and casual. I leaned up and in, motioning for him to kiss me, and he obliged. He was not comfortable with it there in public, I could tell. We sipped our drinks and chatted and watched others dance for a while. Then he took my hand to help me down from the stool and told me to dance with him. He either saw a terrified look on my face, or he sensed my fear because he looked at me sweetly and patiently while he coaxed, *"Don' worry baby, I teach you. Look in my eyes. I am here."*

I felt protected and safe. I danced bachata. It was easy. I was in a dream. He was my Prince Charming. This was my ball, and I was basking in every moment. The night was wonderful for the four of us so far. So, when closing call came, what would we do next? Sandy had it all arranged. I guess she had taken every opportunity to talk to Juliàn and Ian and plan, which was fine with me. I didn't want this night to end. We would all go to my house for coffee. I had never done anything like that before, having near strangers over in the middle of the night, but I was not saying no. This was my chance. Full speed ahead.

We got to my house, and Juliàn immediately asked for sweets. I had some fresh strawberries and whipped cream in the fridge, so I brought them out and began to prepare to serve them. I received strict orders that night that I needed to have a better variety of sweets in the house because "Spanish men love a bite of something sweet after eating." We sipped on hot coffee and nibbled on fresh organic strawberries that I lightly dusted with cinnamon and then drizzled with sweet whipped cream, as we sat talking and laughing in a cozy circle around my kitchen island. I could not believe Juliàn was at my house. He was mine! Well, not technically yet, but I was never into technicalities anyway.

Chapter 17

Secrets

Sometimes secrets are great. You know, something that will make someone happy, like a surprise gift they have been dreaming of that you thoughtfully purchased and carefully hid until the day of the special occasion arrived for you to give it. Other times, secrets are bad. Like when a child is told to keep crucial things from their parents—an inappropriate touch or comment or a problem with another child. But even worse than that is actually *being* a secret. Being a secret can make you feel like a second-class citizen, like you're not good enough to be seen, like you do not even exist. And actually, for the most part, you do not exist, and that is the beginning of a downward spiral that eventually leaves you emotionally discombobulated and very difficult to put back together.

*****

We had been sitting in the car for more than an hour, a habit I was tired of. I mean, I was getting my work done and so was he, but we would sit in my car a lot because we always had to stay close to the clinic he was working in because he was very conscientious when it came to doing his job well. I was not tired of any time spent with him, but I was getting tired of the car. We had been doing this for about three months, and Valentine's Day was coming. I told him how much I wanted him to meet my family and that we should go out to dinner. His response was usually "Maybe" or "Soon," but I wasn't taking no for an answer for this day. I really wanted to be out with him on that special night, and he knew it. I wanted to share the night as a couple with my sister and her husband, so I arranged it with her. It took a lot of convincing to get him to say yes, but I planned it out—the restaurant, the time, and the way we would do it. I was content to go out the evening of the thirteenth because it would be easier to do since it was a Friday night. Valentine's Day would probably be a nightmare, not just because it was Valentine's Day but it was on a Saturday. I was thrilled to celebrate on Valentine's Eve.

Friday came, and I was sooooo excited. Juliàn came to my house right after work. Fridays he was always off by two o'clock, so we got to be home to rest for a while before going to eat. Juliàn kept saying he was tired and just wanted to be with me. He was sitting on my couch, holding me and lightly kissing me, the whole while begging me to cancel our double date with my sister. He was in his work clothes—khakis and a polo shirt—looking so handsome with his tanned, muscular arms. I could not wait to show him off to my family. He started kissing me harder, the way I liked, and begging me more and more to cancel. He insisted that it was too soon and too expensive. I calmed his nerves and said it was too late to cancel. I assured him that we would have fun and that I would give him cash to pay. I did not fully know it then, but it was more than nerves. Juliàn's secret would no longer be a complete secret. He would be exposed to my family. This night was more than just exposing him to my family. I was sure that now he would end his relationship with *her*. He would feel welcomed and comfortable and would see how my family was not judgmental and would freely accept him. He had been telling me that he owed her and that he just needed a little time. I was sure after celebrating Valentine's Day with me, things would change for him. I mean, he picked me over her for the most romantic day of the year. He came after me, right?

We got in my car and went to the bank to get cash to pay for dinner. He did not have enough to cover four dinners in a decent restaurant on a special night and I did, so I thought nothing of it. I gave him the cash, and we went to eat. We arrived and were seated to wait for my sister and her husband. As usual, they were late arriving. We ordered a bottle of Chardonnay and sipped to relax. I was excited, and he was really nervous. I thought his nerves were all about my family, but I now know he was also very worried about *her* at home. His phone vibrated at the moment we shared our first sip of Chardonnay and never really stopped after that. My sister arrived, and she was rushed and smiling; but her husband was his usual guarded, quiet self, and the hello that was exchanged between Juliàn and him was more than awkward. They quickly glanced at the menu and ordered drinks, and there was near silence at the table for far too long. I kept trying to make conversation, but it was really difficult until the men decided to order the same thing and they then began to talk with a bit more ease, and the heaviness lessened. We decided to forgo dessert, say our goodbyes and end the evening. Although the night had improved, the dinner had fallen short. It was awkward and felt so forced. Even though things settled and got more relaxed by the end of it, I regretted it and wished we were alone, and I was very unsure of why it was nothing I dreamt of.

As we pulled up to my house, Juliàn's phone started ringing again. It started before we went to the restaurant and then vibrated on silent throughout the entire meal. He had to answer now. Until then, Juliàn was doing a job of making me forget *she* existed; but that night, it was impossible, especially when he started cursing her existence. He never said cruel things, but that night, he did call her a few Spanish adjectives I understood. Sighing heavily and putting his index finger to his lips in a gesture to keep me quiet, he looked at me and answered the phone. Apologizing and making excuses to her, he called her *baby* and told her, "*Tango langosta,*" explaining in Spanish that he had leftover lobster for her that he saved from a work-related dinner with the guys. I could hear her screaming in Spanish. She was demanding he get there to see her. I felt betrayed and angry. I paid for that lobster he had leftover and he was giving it to *her*? My scallops flipped in my stomach, and I felt a little bit woozy—just a little.

I guess he saw the hurt and anger in my eyes. He touched my face and kissed my cheeks before he kissed me hard on the mouth.

He told me he had fun and then assured me, *"I will call from the car and see you in the morning."*

I pretended everything was fine, but it wasn't. I pretended he was going there to end it with her, but he wasn't. I pretended I was in control and strong and could walk away at any moment, but I couldn't.

Chapter 18

Tropical Hopes

P J (Paulo Junior) was sitting on the front sidewalk of his grand-parents house, more than five thousand miles away from what had been his home for the last twelve years. It was a small, farming town in a well-known state in Brazil, Minas Gerais, with a good reputation and fair representation of the simple life. Life here was easy in contrast to the life which had become very difficult in New Jersey. Sitting next to his Uncle (Tió, pronounced "Cheeo") Marcelo and having a light conversation, PJ was inwardly reflecting on the things that had gone so wrong over the last few years. He had always dreamt of marriage and a strong family, something he knew could be great because of his loving parents and two brothers he was so close to. He grew up learning that the family unit was most important, and he wanted his own loving wife and family as priority, like the family he grew up in. His family lived both here in Minas Gerais then in the fast and crowded city of São Paulo until they all eventually migrated to Newark, New Jersey, where they faced immigrant hardships not well known to most Americans. They had to learn a new language, a new monetary system and a new education system, all while assimilating into a very different culture and way of life.

Now, with an all-too-familiar hot breeze gently blowing and barely touching his moist brow, PJ sat silent, lost in his own thoughts. It was summer here—32 degrees Celsius (98 degrees Fahrenheit). As hot as it was here, PJ thought about just how cold winter was in New Jersey now and how much colder it felt for him to be separated from his wife of just two years and his four-year-old son—the apple of his eye and his personal carbon copy. PJ felt devastated by the broken marriage he was coming out of that he had once vowed to commit to for the rest of his life. He believed with his whole heart that it would last forever. He felt angry but also confused by his soon-to-be ex-wife's decision to destroy their life by betraying him. He was doubtful of who he was and of where he was going. Encouraged by his parents to visit both sets of his grandparents here in Minas, he felt safe. He was far away from the disappointment of his life in this calm and familiar place and he considered moving back.

Looking up as he sat, he could not help but notice what was galloping closer toward him. A beautiful chestnut horse with the most beautiful girl he had seen in some time—five foot eleven inches tall with glistening, sandy-brown hair and long lean legs wrapped around that majestically galloping taxi. In Minas Gerais, it was normal to see horses, bicycles, cars, and people all sharing the same dirt- or stone-covered roads. When PJ looked up to see the most beautiful sight he had seen in a long time, he knew he had to know more about her, and he knew he would soon.

Chapter 19

Boundaries

What we experience in our lives, especially in the early, formative years, sets the foundation for how we live our lives, the good and the bad. As we go through our young lives, we learn the concept of boundaries. When lines are crossed in marriage and we witness it in living color as children, we often feel confused later. The end result is we behave a certain way—the wrong way—because of what we have learned.

I do not say this to excuse any offensive or immoral behavior. I say this to raise awareness. Being touched—violated sexually as a child—by a married, Christian member of the clergy somehow make the lines of relationships very blurry and therefore a bit easier to cross. George's wife and the commitment he made to her was practically nonexistent behind closed doors.

I believe this pattern of behavior, as well as the needs I had, fueled the belief that Juliàn was the one for me. I believed I just had to fight whatever forces were working against me, and this allowed me to fall into things that were wrong. This behavior set me up to sink into a dark pit that I never would have thought possible. It was as though my conscience became seared and the hot iron of life nearly flattened me.

Rules, covenants, commitments have a place and a purpose. They are meant to be followed, respected, and enforced. They are in place to protect us, though we often confuse rules as punishment.

Boundaries are necessary to keep us safe from the oncoming traffic and the out-of-control freight train. We must be taught these boundaries as children, not just in word but also in deed. We must respect them. We must follow them for our own well-being, so the that train doesn't flatten us.

*****

Juliàn and I were in a pattern, a routine. I made him my boyfriend, and I made our relationship "normal" to everyone who asked about my guy. If they were affiliated with work at all, they never saw a picture of him or us together. They just knew I often met him for lunch and heard my frequent calls.

I did a great job of making it all appear so good and so normal. Deep down, I guess I was convincing myself that the things that were happening that were not-so-great and not-so-normal were okay. I called the different things "really special."

We were supposed to go out dancing again—alone. Juliàn promised to hold me close and teach me to bachata better and even to dance mambo (which is basically bachata but a lot faster). I was hesitant to go, but I would do anything for him, especially if I could be with him. He called me early in the evening on the Friday we planned to go out to tell me he had to work. I had been waiting for a call about time and place.

"Hey baby. Ahhhh, can you believe I have to go to the other clinic and close up?" he asked. *"They say no one else can go. What I can do? I can't say no. I could lose my job."*

"It's fine." I said, disappointed, but secretly relieved I did not have to face the dancing chicas again. Closing up a clinic, especially if the system is disinfected, takes about four hours. I knew what was coming next.

"Why don' you yus' come here wit' me? Nobody gonna be here. You can bring dinner, and we can dance bachata alone."

I hated this idea, but at the same time I also loved it. He told me to come around seven. I made a dinner I knew he would love—skirt steak with homemade chimichurri, fresh steamed broccoli drizzled with olive oil and lemon, and creamy mashed potatoes loaded with butter and fresh cream. I packaged his dinner with care and set off to meet him. We met in the parking lot in a centrally located clinic in New Jersey. We danced bachata and mambo with Dominican music blaring from a parked car with doors and windows opened. At that time, I thought it was all very sweet and romantic. We were dancing alone in the dark with parking lights that replaced spotlights. Moments alone in the clinic and hospital parking lots became the routine. At first, it felt so different and so romantic, but those moments eventually stripped me of any dignity I had. I started believing I was just not good enough to be seen in public with him. He repeated over and over again how he was not ashamed of me and that I was beautiful and that we did go out to lunch and dinner a lot in public. I guess my "special" and "secret" dates were just the proverbial handwriting on the wall. I chose only to see that handwriting once in a while until I let it disappear again.

Chapter 20

Dark

Darkness. It is all around me, closing in on me and taking over my space. "Go!" a voice from inside desperately screams, but the darkness is deaf. It does not hear me scream. It is moving in on me like a giant black cloud that overtakes the billowy white clouds during a violent storm. It is suffocating. The storm is here. I am lost on a ship that is carrying me on a vast black ocean until I am completely swallowed up in it. I cannot breathe. I cannot see. I cannot taste. I cannot think. There is no way out. There is no gray, just deep, dark blackness hovering over me, pulling me under. Gurgling, I try, try, try to get up just enough to peek my nose out to catch some air. I just need enough to pull my head out of it to breathe, but my arms are too weak. I am starving. I have no strength. There is no use. The pain is deep. It has numbed me. It has consumed me. It has taken me. There is no point. I give up.

Drifting…thinking…hoping in the darkness. My thoughts are disjointed, like a broken string of pearls scattered all around. I am trying to put the necklace together but the band is broken, and it is so dark. *He DOES love me…he tells me…he holds me…he loves me…I am sure he does.*

He loves her more. Blackness.

I am the one! He will leave her. I know it. He says I am amazing. He just needs time.

He loves her more. Blackness.

He will see me tonight. We can spend all day and have dinner. It will change. He never has dinner with her. Do not give up on this.

He loves her more. Black. Black. Black.

I hate the color of my bedroom. I liked it a lot when it was first done—a trendy salmon, but not too salmon, with just enough low tones to make you like it. I hated it now. It was stuck. It was tired. A cold, dead fish. Listening to him on the phone say the same thing I had been hearing for far too long during our nightly phone conversation, I looked up at the tray ceiling. There, the color was a shade darker—*Wild Alaskan Salmon*. I hated it more.

"I's okay baby. I jus' need time. TIME. Jus' give me a little time. I don' love her."

At that moment, I see a dashing beam of bright light. He says, *"baby."*

I picture his smile. I feel warm and safe…but I really am stuck in the dark, and that flash of light quickly fades. How did I get here? How will I ever leave?? I am sinking, falling, failing. The salmon turns black. Black, black, black.

I had fallen into this cycle of ups and downs and pacifying promises. I was loving every second of laughing and lunch and coffee and steak out on Saturday nights, then hating every second of crying my eyes out knowing he was still with her—*really* with her. Nothing was clear anymore, and none of it made any sense, but I was holding on with all my strength, desperately hoping for the day to come when time had run out for him and he was free to be with me.

I am a person of faith. No, no, no, not *just* a "person of faith" in a polite, religious, do-all-the-right-things kind of way. I live by faith. I walk by faith. I am a faith person. I grew up spending time developing this faith by learning, rehearsing, and believing the Bible which has yet to fail me or anyone who stakes a foundation in it. I have mountain-moving faith in a mountain-moving God, and it is real and it works. I have seen and felt it work, over and over and over. And I *love* the God of that mountain-moving faith because not only can He relate to me, He became me—well, not me, but human flesh. He stepped out of His divine role. Christ put it aside to be birthed through a human and became Jesus, to feel what I feel and live what I live. He did this to identify with every damnable situation I could ever face and then took my place on a cross as my substitute so I would not have to suffer through sin and sickness and spiritual death. So why am I stuck in this hole of darkness when I am a child of the light?

God is definitely *not* mad at me. He is light and good and He loves me, like my daddy loves me but more. He is perfect. He *is* love. His love is perfect. So, why this pain? Why this struggle? The standard response from many is *"God is just teaching you a lesson."* REALLY? Am I that ignorant? Does my father on earth teach me lessons by torturing me? Am I that untaught that I need a lesson that rips me to my core? It is deeper than that. There is much more, and when the blackness fades, I will know. What I am *sure* of now is that GOD did *not* put me here, but He surely will get me out.

Chapter 21

Moving On in Brazil

PJ turned to his Tio Marcelo, and before he could ask who the sandy-haired beauty was, his uncle was talking about her. Small towns are notorious for everyone knowing everything about each other, and this small town in Minas was no exception. Tio Marcelo not only knew about her but about her whole family, and he knew where she lived and how to get his nephew to talk to her. It just so happened that she was selling her house, and Tio and PJ would go look at it and talk to her. After all, PJ was considering moving back to Brazil. He really wanted to go back to São Paulo but maybe he would stay here if things happened to fall into place.

Just a few days later, after traveling a short distance, Tio Marcelo rang her doorbell. Opening the front door, she appeared with a warm smile and a warm Brazilian hello. *"Bom dia. Tudo bem? Eu quero presentar meu sobrinho."*

"Bom dia, prazer," PJ said with a shy smile.

"O prazer é todo meu," she said with confidence, welcoming them in.

The house was beautiful and modern, and PJ was impressed and quiet as she chatted and walked him and his uncle through it. When the twenty-minute tour was over, PJ politely asked for her phone number, explaining that he wanted to discuss the house and the possibility of buying it with his parents. In that small town at that time, the first three digits of everyone's number was the same—only the last four were different. She called out as they left, *"Quatro, um, trés, quatro."*

Smiling to himself, PJ repeated the number out loud back to her first, then to himself over and over—about fifty times until he was back at his grandmother's home and sure he would never forget it.

Chapter 22

Perspective

Why does morning come so fast? Why is it that you can go to sleep at eleven at night and wake up seven hours later tired and thinking you have only been asleep for a few minutes? How come when we take a seven-day vacation to a paradise, we feel like it only lasted a day? Why does the Monday workday feel so long and exhausting? A minute with a person you do not like can feel like hours while days in the arms of a lover can feel like minutes. Perspective—the way we view a situation—the appearance of things relative to the person viewing them and where they are.

There are times in life when we tolerate things for way too long because we lose perspective. We resent situations we often create on our own and then struggle to be free from them. Maybe, if we take time to change our viewpoint, to get a different perspective on the situation, we can turn it around. For instance, when I am standing inside a gated area at the bottom of a hill, I will never be able to fully assess what is going on above me. This is one reason we need others in our lives who love and care for us. Their vantage point is different. They can see the dangers coming toward us. Their viewpoint is not from within, it is from without. Often, our family and friends have a view not unlike one at the top looking down, seeing what we cannot see.

When we fight the people who love us, those who are watching and listening and warning us of the dangers ahead, we are destined to experience what feels like a lifetime of pain. It is so valuable to be quiet and listen and borrow the eyes of others. It can save us a lot of heartache.

*****

We were sitting in Liberty Park at lunchtime in late spring. The sun was yellow and warm, teasing us that summer had arrived. We munched on delicious deli sandwiches while watching the beautiful, shiny new buildings and the boats cruising by on the New Jersey side of the Hudson River. Juliàn got a call. It was a custom now, especially at lunchtime, and I was used to it. This time he left the car abruptly. He was yelling in Spanish, and although I could understand some of it, I did not get much. Juliàn rarely got loud or angry, so I paid closer attention, knowing this was something serious. I rolled the window down to hear as much as I could. He was telling her he was done. He was telling her he was tired and that he never asked for this and that he did not want her. I could barely believe my ears, but I was sure: he was letting her go. *(I knew he would!)*

Juliàn came back to the car and told me everything that happened. He was annoyed for the first few minutes while he ranted and raved and explained that he was tired of her mouth and her attitude. He explained that he had had enough of her questions and nagging and that she failed in her attempt to control him. After his rant, he turned full faced toward me, put up his hands, walked toward me and the car, and said the words I longed to hear.

"I'm all yours, baby! I tol' you! I told you I jus' needed time." With a broad, crooked smile and a look of freedom and excitement I had not seen, eyes twinkling, he grabbed me and hugged and kissed me.

I could not believe my ears. *Oh my God,* I thought! The ecstasy of the moment! I wanted to call my doubting friends (the few who knew) and scream, *"See? I told you!"* I wanted to jump on top of the Statue of Liberty, which was in sight and pretty close, and shout it from the torch! Instead, I kissed him back, elated, and we celebrated and snuggled and kissed, enjoying the moment as I secretly made plans for our future in my head.

Later, I did call a few of my friends. I sensed shock and disbelief—not stated, just felt—through the phone. Lisa was happy, telling me she was, and then asking me, *"Don't you feel great?"*

Anna was happy too, but more reserved about it with an, *I hope he does not disappoint you again* sort of tone with a lot of *"uh-huhs"*, and *"yeahs"*. I did not care that Anna was jaded. I was so happy. I called Ian, and he was pretty excited too. It was his idea to go out and celebrate right away. That night, Juliàn, Ian, and I went out to a small jazz cafe in the trendy, college town of Montclair to celebrate. The food tasted so good and went down so easy. The night was light and fresh with what felt like total freedom. I felt confident in that moment. Who cared what my friends thought? I knew he loved me. I knew this would happen. He was *the one.*

*****

One week of pure peace and bliss. Juliàn was all mine, no distractions, no concerns. After that week, I guess her anger wore off and the phone calls resumed. Our bliss soon became our agony as she insisted that "no matter what," they were getting back together. He owed her. At least that is what he said she said, and I knew that deep down, he believed that.

Juliàn and I never even had a consecutive hours' worth of peace. She called and called and called in relentless pursuit of him, like a hungry cheetah hunting its prey. Her catch was in sight, and she was not stopping to rest. When he didn't answer her after a few days of phone calls, she showed up on his doorstep and began watching his every move. I was never at his place. He had moved a few times, and he had invited me when we first met because he lived alone, but I never felt comfortable. At this point, he did not really want me to see his not-so-great apartment, which he rented with a few other guys in a not-so-great neighborhood on a not-so-great street where I had been many times with him.

Juliàn began to get concerned because he knew that she could be emotional and angry and sometimes act on an impulse. During this time of their breakup, he left my house around nine at night, concerned of what she was doing or where she might be. He was afraid if she did not see him go home at a decent hour, she might do something *really* crazy.

He usually called me from the road immediately after leaving my house because he knew I felt sad, and then again from bed before falling off to sleep. That night, I waited until around 2:00 a.m to hear his ringtone.

"Heyyyyyy. I'm so tiyrrred. That lady, she was at my door when I pulled up. My roommates said she sat on the steps waiting for me all day until I got home. That lady—she crazy! You don' mess wit' her. She tol' me I owe her and she gonna marry me even if we are divorced in week."

Crying and shaking and hoping to get through to him, I said deliberately and firmly but with some restraint (he didn't need two crazy women in his life), *"Tell her you found someone else!"* I started to lose it a little; getting louder, I continued, *"Tell her you don't want her! Don't let her do this! I will be with you. She will give up if you just don't give in! We can deal with this. My family will help us!"*

He answered, *"I know, I know, baby. I got such a headache right now. I am so tired. Please let me sleep. I talk to you tomorrow."*

"I love you. I LOVE you. We can get through this."

"Okay. Goo' nigh'."

Morning came so slow. I was up and ready to go really early. I got Juliàn coffee and some breakfast like usual and waited in our spot for him. I was determined to be the strength he needed to end this once and for all. He pulled up, got out of his car and into mine smiling widely at me. He kissed me, sipped his coffee said, *"Thank you, baby,"* then picked up right where he left off the night before.

"What I can do, baby? That lady, she is CRAZY. She called her mother an' my mother an' my sister to have a meeting. I have to go. I's disrespectful not to."

She had it all arranged. A family meeting with the parents to put him back in his place as her boyfriend and give him perspective. Who has a family meeting about a relationship that isn't even official? I was barking mad, red hot—*livid*. I was stronger than her and a whole lot smarter. I could fix this.

"DON'T GO! What's wrong with you? Do you want to be stuck with her? Don't you have a mind? Don't show up, and they will realize you are not for her or with her. You even told me your mother doesn't like her or her family! What is wrong with you?"

He spoke a lot of words but said nothing. He did a lot of "You're right" and "Mm-hmmm" and "I know." I am sure I was the winning lawyer arguing my case for him too. My parents told me for years that I should have been a lawyer, and deep down I knew they were right because I could pick a side and argue a case like the best of 'em. But what's the use of a having a Park Avenue law firm when someone doesn't care if he wins his case? Juliàn went to that "meeting." I knew when and where it was and was pretty tempted to interrupt it, but I knew I could not fix it. *He* had to fix it. *He* had to stand up and tough it out, but he did not and *POOF*, just like that, they were back together.

I still believed Juliàn was the one for me and that it was simply a matter of time and destiny. After all, the greater the resistance, the better the story, the stronger the bond, right? When we talked about "the meeting," he insisted this was just a temporary solution to shut her up and calm things down.

"Don' worry, baby. I'm not really with her. She just thinks I am. I's temporary. I need a better way to end it. I will."

My sea of disappointment and despair began to get blacker and deeper because he knew how to tell me it was temporary. He knew how to tell me he was going to end up with me and that he was young and to just be patient. He knew when to calm me and when to plan something a little bit more special to keep me happy. But I knew I was sinking fast, and I was not willing to let anyone throw me a lifeline. I pushed my friends away more and more, isolating myself and limiting my time out of my house to him and his friends.

"What is wrong with me?" I questioned. "I am strong," I reasoned. "I don't need him," I tried to convince myself. But I was not strong at all, and I did need him. I let him define who I was, how I could be loved, and how I should love, and that was just plain dangerous. I believed he did not love her. I believed he had to come up with a better way to end it. So I carried on with him, as if nothing was wrong. I believed he was the one for me.

In the midst of all of my relationship woes, I was doing really well professionally. I had managed to buy a great town home and furnish it beautifully. I longed to share it with someone, but I settled for exotic fish in a saltwater aquarium as my company most times. I had almost completely stopped being with my many different friends. We no longer had much to talk about because they were mostly silent when it came to my relationship or they were very judgmental. So I spent a lot of time home alone with my fish. They were beautiful and fairly easy to care for once acclimated to the tank. It was calming to watch them glide through the water so effortlessly, each one unique and colorful and special. I spent a lot of time learning about saltwater fish and the classes of fish that you could carefully combine and the best way to feed them. I purchased anemones and marveled at their strength in a new environment, being shipped so carefully from the West Coast. It was a good hobby to dive into and escape the sadness in my small world.

As much as I was letting go of fun with friends, right around this time I met some people at church that I had an interest in getting to know. Actually, they were sort of persistent in getting to know me, and their timing was pretty good. They were a married couple from Brazil, who recently moved to New Jersey; Lorenzo and Gabby. He was a former soccer player who was learning English from his pretty and patient wife and teacher. They had spoken to me at church a few times, and he told me that he was able to do tile work and other handyman side jobs and was doing them for a few other people at church. I wanted a small decorative job done in my kitchen, so I invited them over to discuss it.

Lorenzo and Gabby stopped by on a cold midweek evening to talk about my kitchen. I made some coffee and served some bakery dessert as we got to know each other better. Lorenzo gulped down crisp, cold Coca-Cola, saying with gratitude that it was "from God." He devoured the delicious cream-and-fresh-fruit-layered torte that I served while Gabby and I chatted politely and sipped coffee. The conversation revealed they had recently moved to a new apartment and needed furniture. When I learned this, instinctively I offered them a barely used chaise couch I had on my first floor. I told them it was theirs if they came and got it and moved my other couch down into its place. We went downstairs to see it.

"Really? You will give this to us?" Lorenzo asked in disbelief.

"As long as you come and get it and move my other couch downstairs, sure."

Resourceful Lorenzo arranged to be at my house the very next day after five. He planned to bring two friends. I said that was fine, knowing the next night was a night Juliàn usually came over for a late dinner.

At about five thirty the next day, my doorbell rang, and Lorenzo brought and introduced me to two of his coworkers: Kevin, an American who I knew for a long time from church and was surprised but happy to see and PJ, a handsome Brazilian with light-brown eyes, a soft kind voice, and an obviously athletic body covered in some trendy clothes. I tried my best to avoid looking into the sparkly, observant Brazilian eyes of a man I had met for the first time. I reminded myself of Juliàn, who would be over later that night. I was acutely aware of their similar look. They even had tattoos in the same place, on the same bronzed and buffed left arm. Juliàn's arm boasted his own name in messy block letters in the colors of the Dominican flag. PJ's tattoo read, "Jesus." It was black and neatly scripted over a music staff. I made a quick mental note and ordered pizza, but not just any pizza. I ordered a grandma's special pizza complete with fresh mozzarella and delicious marinara resting on top of that buttery, delicious cheese. I knew the guys would work up an appetite because both couches were very heavy and awkward to carry. When the pizza arrived and we sat at my kitchen island to eat, PJ was so gracious after taking his first bite. *"Now this is real pizza,"* he mused. *"Nothing like the garbage they order at work every Saturday."* I smiled, raised my eyebrows, and shook my head in agreement, avoiding those kind eyes of his but secretly happy he enjoyed it. A compliment to an Italian about the food you serve is almost a sacred thing. We do not take it lightly, though we always pretend we do.

Juliàn arrived so late that evening that I could barely stay awake. He had to disinfect one of the bigger systems, and it took longer than he expected. I was happy he came but so mad that I could not even enjoy his company. I was too tired to even talk, and I knew morning would come fast and I had to wake up and leave early to beat traffic. I noticed his tattoo and secretly remembered PJ's.

The next morning, I woke up tired thinking I needed rest but realizing I did not get much. Another day of the same routine came and went and a few weeks went by. I did begin to spend a little time with Lorenzo and Gabby. They were grateful for the couch and constantly inviting me over. I enjoyed their company. Our lives were similar before I let Juliàn take over my life. To be content, I tried to focus on the good feelings when Juliàn and I were together, which was pretty much every day during the day. His calling me every opportunity he had and seeing me every free moment reinforced what he said. He loved me. He wanted me. She was going away. It was just a matter of time. I still felt sad and alone most nights and on weekends if I didn't see him, but I was managing to get by. He succeeded in making me forget all the bad. I still cannot understand how he could spend so much time with me and have her. We spent so much free time together. Every weekday, it was breakfast, lunch, and dinner with very few exceptions. I worked around our meetings every day, and I worked hard and did my job well all week. Friday nights, Saturday mornings, and many Sunday afternoons we spent together. He had to love me. He had to be trapped by her craziness, like he said. She was a strong girl with a mean streak and a domineering nature. I witnessed it after all. She stalked him, called relentlessly, spoke *at* him—not *to* him—loudly. He even worried that she might do something desperate to herself, him, or worse. He was the victim trapped in a desperate struggle to leave a crazy girl—like the Lifetime movies on cable. The ones where the poor girl ends up going insane or worse. The only problem was, this was not Lifetime. It was not television. It was not a movie. This was *my* life, *my* sanity, *my* future, *my* destiny.

My good friends were still in my life, but I saw them less frequently. Debby, Lisa C, Lisa D, and Anna were slow to give me any

advice, cautious about the entire situation, and doubtful of his intentions. These relationships became somewhat strained, so I chose the
comfort of our routine coffee, lunches, kissing, and losing perspective. This philosophy came complete with Friday night free-for-alls,
Saturday outings with Ian, and Sunday afternoons for lunch. I was
consumed with Juliàn. He had become my life. Nothing else really
mattered. I was going through the motions of life. It was a dangerous and ill-fated decision that I seemed to have made without full
awareness.

One afternoon in the car, Juliàn told me about how he and
Ian were planning to go to the Dominican Republic for a few days
for vacation and to see family. He told me how much he missed it
and how beautiful it was and that he wanted me to come. Over the
next few months before the trip, they both kept asking me to go. I
considered it, but I was too embarrassed to go on what I perceived to
be a trip full of perfect chicas with perfect bodies on perfect beaches
speaking Spanish. I could not deal with all that or with the uncer-
tainty of where I would be sleeping, so I told him I would wait for
him. I did not need that kind of pain, and besides, I could not lie to
my family about who I was going with. When the day came, I said
good-bye, gave Juliàn some cash to buy me some jewelry, wished
them well, and waited to hear of their safe landing back home.

The trip seemed uneventful, and I was glad he was having fun
with Ian and not *her*. He called me twice from there. I thought that
was very sweet. Their return came more quickly than I expected.
I was excited to see Juliàn and what kind of jewelry he had gotten
me. After all, I had given him some money for his trip—a generous
amount of money and he promised me something special. He knew
I had gotten some silver jewelry on the beaches of Mexico, and I was
sure he looked for something like that but better.

I was waiting anxiously in the parking lot of Dunkin' Donuts.
He pulled up next to me and smiled. My stomach felt like I was in
a roller-coaster car going up the track. Oh, that sexy smile of his! I
couldn't wait to kiss it.

He got out of his car and into mine. He was a little tanner and smiling widely he was saying, "Hellooo," long and sweetly and hugging and kissing me the same way. How I missed him!

He pulled out a key chain with a DR logo on a little drum. It was cute, and I said that. Then he pulled out another box, I was sure it was a ring or at least a bracelet. Excitedly, I opened the box expecting to see a beautiful, thoughtful present. I was wrong. It was a colored, decorative plate with the country logo on it. You know, the kind of thing you buy for the aunt you really don't like last minute at the airport, before you get on the plane.

He could tell I was disappointed, and it precipitated the first real fight and the first time I really tried to walk away from him for good.

"Are you serious?" I blurted out angry and loud. *"A PLATE!?"*

"What, you don' like it? I's for your house. I's my country colors and shape. I got it for your counter to always think of me. If you do not like, I mean, I understand but is not nice of you." He was so good at this stuff. A professional at being the jerk but making me feel like I was.

"What did you get her?" I asked in a sarcastic outrage. *"Because I'm sure is wasn't a DISH. She would throw it in your face."*

"Nothing! NOT'ING! You crazy?? I got her nothing."

I did not believe him, and I was sure he spent money on her. He tried to interrupt me, but I was mad, and I was crying. I felt so stupid and so unspecial. I felt rejected. It really wasn't about the gift. I was starting to see the truth. I asked him to get out of the car, but he wouldn't leave. He touched me in ways he knew I responded to and assured me that he "ran out of money" and that he "helped his family there" and that I should be patient because I was the best thing ever in his life and soon he would be free. I insisted he leave. I felt so stupid. He left, and I cried for a long time. I was getting used to these ups and downs, but they were affecting me more than I realized. My cries became sobs. I was not sure what was worse—what just happened, or what would happen if I let him go.

I didn't talk to him for a few days. He called a lot, but I did not care. After the sting of what happened softened a little, and a few more days passed, I saw him at work, and he followed me to the parking lot. I wanted to be strong enough to let go, but I missed him so much. He said all the right things, and I forgave him, and it felt so good to be with him. Nothing else mattered. I was not the kind of girl who needed gifts anyway. I was the giver.

Chapter 23

Josianne

Standing at the front door he remembered so well, PJ waited for Josianne to answer. Smiling carefully not to reveal too much excitement as she stepped out, he grabbed the door as he watched her thinking how beautiful she was. A flower was waiting on the passenger side seat. She knew immediately it was for her as she thanked him with enthusiasm and secured her seat belt. PJ planned to take a forty-minute ride to another town to grab some ice cream and chat, far from the familiarity of this town and the gossip that would come soon enough at the sight of them together. They spent most of the night savoring homemade ice cream and talking a lot about life. They talked and walked and shared past sad relationship experiences, the whole time enjoying the newness of each other and planning the rest of the week. PJ spent each night planning what they would do until he had to leave for his home in New Jersey at the end of the week.

On one of those shared evenings, sitting in a familiar modest restaurant, (the only kind of restaurants that were available there) PJ put some rice and beans on his plate and asked Josianne if she wanted some while they waited for the best part of the meal—traditional churrasco. Pronounced 'shoe-has-ko', this is a celebration of grilled meats and chicken that has helped make Brazilian food quasi famous. Each type of meat is grilled on a huge skewer and when ready to eat, brought table side and sliced onto a special plate. It is a paced, parade of perfectly grilled top sirloin steak, skirt steak, beef ribs, pork ribs, sausages, chicken hearts, chicken legs and more and is traditional all over the country. Accepting this kind gesture and immediately noticing his sweetness, she began to talk about her simple life there and continued to inquire about his life so far away and how life was in America. Their connection was strong, and PJ was sure it could get stronger, thinking she was just the thing he needed to put his life back on track and keep him in his native country. As the various meats began to be sliced directly onto their plates, the conversation became more comfortable. PJ and Josianne both felt this was what they wanted and needed. She talked about life so simple and so sweet, and when it was time to go home, neither wanted to. They walked and talked on the dark quiet streets until they could talk no more. When he dropped her off at her door, he asked if he could call her again in the morning and every morning. *"Com certeza,"* she said with a smile and softly kissed him good-night.

Chapter 24

Up and Down

Sometimes we can be so limited in our thinking. Our minds confine us to constricted borders because of past experiences and failures. "I am down on my luck." Have you ever heard this? Have you ever said it? Forget about saying it, have you ever been there, for real?

Life is full of stressors—events that attempt to put us down and keep us there. "I am stressed," has become such a part of the modern vernacular that it has almost made being stressed something to look forward to. We just expect stress to hinder us. We allow stress to inhibit us from moving to the next level. It is time to change this mentality.

Although it is true that we feel stress on many different levels for many different reasons, how we approach it and handle it is the key. In the words of my incredible dad, there are really only two positions in life: up and getting up. I, for one, am not content to stay down. Change your approach to *down* and realize it is a simple but truly profound difference to say, "I am getting up."

*****

I was sort of tired of hearing my friends' opinions of Juliàn. They didn't really know him and what was going on between us. They didn't feel what we felt. I did not need their approval, so I spoke with them less and less. I did not need anyone else. My dad had always been my best friend, and always in my corner. He loved me and supported me. I left a lot of details out about what was really happening in my life. No one needed to worry about me, especially not my daddy. I had learned to let my dad pray without telling him too much. Thank God for him and his love and faith. I am sure his prayer of faith helped to get me through what was ahead.

It was a typical Tuesday morning, I had made several stops in other cities making patient rounds in many clinics. I walked into the clinic Juliàn was working in. I had walked in there a lot, and today was no different. No one knew we were together. I was a secret, and I made it okay. I compromised all I knew to keep him. My life was my business, especially with work acquaintances. They did not need to know about my life, and I did not want to know about theirs. Ophelia jumped up to say hello to me. After the day she offered to go out and bachata with us, I had started talking with her and texting her a little bit. She was bubbly and charismatic and always very funny. She was also Puerto Rican, very familiar with the Latino culture and apt to discuss it. I needed her insight. Juliàn walked quickly by us both and said hello casually. When he was gone, she leaned in close to me and blurted it out.

"Hey, girl! Did you hear the news? Juliàn got engaged!"

Silence. The room spun around me. I felt sick. I thought I would collapse, but I knew I couldn't. I was there to take care of people, not get sick. I was ready to vomit, and as my respirations increased I felt my heart racing. I tried to ignore it, like I didn't care, and I excused myself, barely making it out the door before tears rushed out of my eyes streaming down my cheeks with rage. This can't be happening to me. I am not this girl! Safe in my car but sick to my stomach, I began to sob. Deep, guttural bursts of devastation were coming from inside. Black tears streaked my face, and I could barely see.

By that time Juliàn realized I had left, and I guess he was confused. I never left without a plan for lunch. He called me. Confused, he asked, *"Hey, baby, where are you? Why did you leave?"*

In an emotional rage I screamed, *"You got ENGAGED? Engaged? You lying, cheating, scheming piece of dirt! YOU LIAR! Liar! How could you do this to me? I hate you! I HATE you!"*

"Wha'? Who tol' you dat?? Wha's wrong wit' you, baby? She's a liar! A gossip! I's no' true. I's not true. Listen to me. I got her a ring before I left to DR, to keep her quiet. My friend have a store. It cost nothing. I's no' an engagement ring! I swear to God!"

I was listening closely. I hung up the phone and went home to cry to my pillow. He swore to God.

Later that night, lying in bed, eyes swollen and feeling a little guilty for not answering his calls, I decided to call Ian. Ian had become my friend too, and he hated *her*. He said what Juliàn always told me was true. He really loved me. He did not love *her*, and he really did just need time. I believed Ian. You would have too.

"Is it true, Ian? Did he get engaged?"

He sounded stunned and a bit confused, and then he said, *"I don't know about that. I know he loves you, but I don't know anything about a ring, sweetie."*

So now I was really confused. I was hearing on a daily basis from Juliàn and every weekend from Ian how much he loved me and wanted me and how much of a witch she was.

It can't be true. Ophelia likes to talk. I thought. So I chose to ignore the flashing yellow sign and I did *not* proceed with caution. I just proceeded.

In the next few days, confused but completely lost in my own feelings for him, I called Anna to tell her everything. I was desperate, and she usually didn't judge. I needed her honesty. Besides, she could help me fix this.

"You know what, Cyn? He is a jerk and a liar. I liked him at first, and I was patient. Are you serious? Now it is time for you to wake up and realize what is going on. You're so much better than this. Why can't you see how great you are?"

I thought about Anna and when we met in physician assistant school. I LOVED her from the first time we spoke. She was smart and very pretty with warm inviting eyes and a sweet, nervous giggle that never came across as nervous, but I knew it was. We became friends immediately. She was a first-generation Italian American—spoke the language and all—and that just made me love her more. We saw each other daily in school, studied together at least three times a week, shared lunches and food-exploring adventures from Brooklyn to Staten Island and New Jersey. We capped off almost every night with a late-night phone call complete with a wrap-up discussion of the day's events, a list of our current fears, and past passions and quotes from any random Seinfeld episode complete with belly laughter that brought us to tears. She was a very special person in my heart. This friendship survived relentless classroom hours, way too many clinical practice rounds, dinner outings, graduation, job hunting, working our first and second professional jobs, Anna getting engaged three times (and finally marrying) and so many more things in our lives. We continued our tradition of speaking for hours every night for years. We laughed and talked about the men in (and out) of our lives, our families, and our dreams. She was my friend.

As time moved on, Anna got involved in a relationship with a successful younger guy. I compared it to mine, but it was very different. She was all about no compromise, and compromise was all I knew. She held her tongue and supported my pursuit for a long time until she could hold it no longer. Our friendship started to crumble. It almost didn't survive because of Juliàn, because of me.

The thing I loved about Anna from the time I met her was her fire. She was so easygoing and fun, but she had a confidence she didn't always reveal to everyone, and I loved it. She had the perfect balance of beauty and a sense of humor, but she was a tough, confronting, Brooklyn girl who would never let you step on her or her loved ones. NEVER. No matter what it cost her, she would pay.

Her voice got louder and higher, and the pace of what she said sped up with intensity. *"You are amazing. You are one of the most amazing people I've ever met. You have helped me out of every problem. You are so much better than this. He's not gonna leave her, Cyn! You know this. Even if he does, you are so much better... What else will it take?"*

I fainted inside, swallowed hard. Then I shook myself. I had to let her know I WAS IN CONTROL.

Calmly and collected, I said, *"I hear you, Annie, but you don't know her. She has him trapped. She threatens him. She's crazy."*

"Mmmhmmm. I guess she has to. She knows him. Whatever, Cyn, if this is what you choose, I cannot stop you. I love you. I do not like it, but I love you. You deserve so much more. If only you could see that..."

She had this ability to drop word bombs and make you think and then pick up and start talking about Seinfeld episodes like that serious conversation of a few minutes ago did not really happen. But we both knew it did. We just moved ahead of it. We laughed about Seinfeld, quoted a few lines as usual, and said good-night. But those moments became less and less frequent, and I fell deeper into the pit of despair, separating myself from every good thing I knew.

Chapter 25

Five Thousand Miles Isn't Enough

PJ had been back home in New Jersey for two weeks, spending most of his time with his son and contemplating when he would return to Minas.

After two weeks, he boarded the plane and began the familiar ten-hour night flight back to Brazil. Arriving solo in São Paulo, PJ rented a car and drove twelve hours directly to Minas to see the girl he was missing. When he arrived back to this familiar place, he went directly to her. Josianne and PJ had been spending a lot of time together. They had just finished attending a family wedding, and although the relationship was going well, there was a level of discomfort PJ was feeling but could not understand.

Early in the mornings, he would go to the lake close to his grandmother's house and think about the things he longed for—a relationship with a woman who was close to God and who understood his desire to serve God in a bigger way. He wanted a woman who could bring out all the qualities he kept deep inside. In those mornings, he would communicate his desires to His God with the assurance it would happen.

Walking and talking in the quiet country streets by day and enjoying life as a new couple, Josianne and PJ planned to visit São

Paulo and meet his family. Although she was beautiful and a very kind person he quieted the longing inside he had for a woman with a deeper connection to the things of God. Shutting off his mind that was fighting this relationship just a little bit, they made plans to make the twelve-hour trip to São Paulo so she could meet his cousins and his Tia Jô.

The ride was long but relaxing, and Tia Jô welcomed her nephew with *pudim*—freshly made custard with a caramel sauce, sort of like flan but with a firmer texture and more flavor (at least according to every Brazilian I know). Pudim is to Brazilians what apple pie is to Americans. It is familiar comfort, a national treasure, and Tia Jô's is amazing! The family warmly welcomed a new, pretty face and hoped for the best for their beloved PJ as they laughed and ate and sipped strong coffee (cafezinha) to balance that sweet buttery custard and got to know one another.

Making the trip back to Minas after a few weeks in São Paulo, the new unofficial official couple spent the next month together. Although PJ loved the fun and fellowship and enjoyed the laughs with her, he had a continual unrest, and although he tried hard to soothe his screaming fears, he could not.

Boarding the plane to go back to his home, PJ thought about his future and hoped he could go back just a little bit, to his past—his few months spent as a happily married man—and as the plane began to ascend, he closed his eyes and dreamed.

Chapter 26

Your Future Is Bright

"*Your future is a whole lot better than your past. I'm in it, and I'm looking in your eyes.*" Those big beautiful, confident, shiny, light-brown, sparkly eyes just a shade darker than hazel-colored opened wide right in front of my face as he gently shook his head up and down, reaffirming his love and commitment to our destiny together. At one time, I had trouble holding that gaze. Not anymore. This is my husband. He moved gently to whisper in my ear.

"*I love you so much. You are my precious gift from God. I do not know how I lived before you, and I cannot see my life without you.*" He whispered so softly, his lips brushing my ear just enough to give me goose bumps all over.

I always thought I would love harder, hold on tighter, say how much in love I was more and overall be on the receiving end less. His love is a friendly, competitive contest of who can love harder. We are committed to this gift of love, and if one of us has a momentary lapse in judgment, we are quick to remind the other of this wonderful gift. Apologies are usually fast and mutual. We agree that life is too precious and too short to waste any more time.

This kind of love is from God. This kind of love *is* God. This kind of love leads, caresses, encourages, corrects, and heals. This kind of love is rare, and we all deserve it. I am just blessed enough to have found it and recognize it.

*****

"I love you, Juliàn."

"I love you too," he replied matter-of-factly with a quick, difficult smile, as he turned his eyes away faster than he should have. A reply was the only way I heard this, and I had to force him to look in my eyes, but I accepted it that way. After all, he did say he loved me. Who was I to judge exactly how he said it? I now felt myself identifying with people's predicaments with a little bit more compassion than before. I felt myself sinking into a murky lake of compromise and I knew—deep, deep down inside—that the more I compromised to keep what I thought I wanted, the faster I would lose it. I was holding on so tightly that I was losing my grip. As much as I pushed away what I knew was talking to me deep down inside, I reasoned that it was still nice to hear "I love you," even if it was a knee-jerk response, even if it was not as sincere as I deserved.

I began to accept a whole lot of things that I had previously advised many, many other people never to settle for. I was a champion counselor to those in hurting relationships and always advised, *"You don't need this. You're bigger and stronger and there are a lot of men out there!"* But somehow, I just did not ever believe those things to be true for me. I believed this was it. I believed it would get better. All great relationships have huge obstacles to overcome and a great love story to tell. I could get through this.

We were working on dinner together on a hot summer weeknight after work. Juliàn loved meat, so I always had a lot ready to prepare. I was in the kitchen cutting fresh Jersey tomatoes, and he was on the deck grilling a few different marinated meats when the doorbell rang. It was Lorenzo and Gabby, stopping by to say hello. Lorenzo had offered to tile my kitchen backsplash as a thank you for the couch I had given them. Since doing the tile, he and Gabby had come to my house a few times spontaneously, and tonight happened to be one of those nights. I was so happy. I had told them about

Julián and how I wanted them to meet him and to spend an evening with another couple. I knew they were a good example for Julián. They seemed to have a great relationship, and they were committed Christians, who were a lot of fun and were not American. Besides, they were eager to meet the "Dominican guy" I could not stop talking about and was practicing my Spanish for (though Lorenzo insisted that I switch to learning Portuguese instead).

Lorenzo and Gabby arrived to witness the feast we were busy preparing, and I insisted they stay and have dinner with us. This was all impromptu. Of course it had to be because I was never really able to plan anything. Lorenzo, a handsome, confident and charismatic twenty-eight-year-old soccer player turned preacher, was his usual bold, confrontational self that night. We were all devouring perfectly grilled skirt steak, baby lamb chops, and Italian sausage with garlicky tomato and string bean salad and homemade coleslaw. Sipping his icy Coke, Lorenzo got straight to the point.

"So, this is your princess, huh guy?" he asked Julián, gesturing toward me. Gabby laughed sweetly, nervously, with her mouth closed as she was chewing a bite of meat. I blushed a little then stopped and looked right into Julián's eyes.

"Of course she is," he obliged and chuckled looking briefly at me and then down to his plate. Lorenzo tried to talk more, but Julián skillfully and quickly ended that subject. He was gentle and soft-spoken and never disrespectful, but he got out of it talking about church and work and Brazil and Portuguese and anything but our relationship. Dinner ended and my new friends left. Julián's relief was palpable, and he said he had fun, but I knew Lorenzo saw without seeing.

Lorenzo called me the next day. From the moment he met me, he seemed to have become my advocate. He did not ask my permission, and he did not struggle to let me know that he was unsure of my relationship. I guess this was partially because Julián was not a churchgoer, but Lorenzo was sort of "tuned in" to me. He just had a feeling. It didn't take much for him to say what he thought.

"Sis, you sure this guy loves you? Maybe you should let go of him. You are going to find someone who loves you the way you deserve to be loved." He said this very seriously, and then he continued with a

lighthearted tone, but I knew he meant what he said next, *"You need a good Brazilian."*

I laughed and shrugged him off. I did not believe that I "deserved to be loved." I wanted to believe I could be loved better, but I did not. I wanted the relationship they seemed to have, but I was content with Juliàn, and I was sure our love and relationship would grow. I was okay to accept the leftover crumbs I was devouring from starvation instead of moving on to the steakhouse. I tried to convince myself this was better. I reasoned that I had none of the garbage people dealt with in "traditional" relationships, and when the day came for the next step, it would be easy.

"He loves me, Lorenzo. I know he does. He needs time to prove it to everyone. He is shy, and he is trapped in some things, and I believe him. You don't have to, I do."

My friend stayed quiet. I appreciated that. We hung up, but I knew Lorenzo was not done, and I am sure I secretly appreciated it.

Juliàn had been telling me how *she* rescued him from a basement apartment and a bed without sheets and a hungry belly. He talked about how they were friends of friends and he really wasn't attracted to her and he really didn't want to be with her and how he resisted it a long time. Then the mutual friends—all aware of her desire for him—helped make something happen one night. He elaborated about how he resisted and resisted but that she was a nice person and "what could it hurt?" He could not get away—not yet.

After I heard that story the first time, I asked him to tell me again and again. I was secretly checking if he changed any of it. He did not. He was always quick to explain. He was quick to answer my questions, and that just made me feel good. I felt in control. After all, I knew everything about *her*, and she knew nothing about me. She would be gone soon. I was sure. The only problem was, for the time being, she was still there. Summer was here, and I had a lot of plans for us that did not include *her*. He had had enough time.

Lorenzo and Gabby were becoming more of a part of my life, though it was separate from Juliàn. Gabby asked if I met his family and if they liked me and how we got along. When I said 'NO,' so aggressively she crinkled her nose and asked, "Why not?" I smiled and shook my head and dodged answering her, saying they lived in Queens and we were "taking our time." I knew it was enough for her to let it go, though she did say he should be proud of me. Lorenzo was more like a bulldog. If he grabbed on, he did not let go, and he began to notice that I was not as happy as I made it seem. They were always trying to get together with me, and I was always making excuses until I got frustrated and blurted out to Lorenzo on a phone call with him that Juliàn "had someone else but was going to end it."

I knew Lorenzo did not buy that. He was Juliàn's age, but from a different time. He was old-school about this subject and noncompromising. I am sure he sensed that I let that slip and felt embarrassed and afraid to bring shame to my father, but Lorenzo was cool about it and promised to keep my secret, and he started to become very instrumental in my life. He kept calling me *sis* and telling me all the good he saw in me—leadership, kindness, intelligence. I did not pay attention to that at the time. It did not matter to me.

As time went by, I did notice that Lorenzo seemed to always know when I was struggling and he was quick to reach out every time. Thank God for the bulldogs in life that get a hold of your coattail and don't let go. You never know when you will need to be rescued.

Chapter 27

Dirt

Sometimes I feel like I am a person buried in the ground, quite the way one buries a dead person. Life is nothing that I hoped for, and things do not work out the way I planned. Everything seems to go wrong, and the pressure of multiple bad situations in my life—relationships, finances, health status—close in on me like dirt all around, pushing in against me. I feel suffocated. Air is not in my lungs like it should be—it feels tight, and it is hard to breathe. It feels like this dirt is designed to take whatever life is in me out of me. But I am not dead, and I am not buried. I am a seed planted in dirt. I am in this deep, dark, place that I may confuse with being buried, but I draw nutrients from the soil that will make me grow. I will draw from the storms that dump rain into the soil for my benefit. This dirt will press in on me and even make me question why I am in this deep, dark, terrible place. But one day at the right time, at just the right moment, I, a planted seed, will break through my own seal, pushing through the dirt, and will begin to grow a root. It will continue to draw from the earth until it grows and surfaces as an amazing fruit—sweetened and perfected and ripe for the picking because it passed the time and tempering tests and saw things for what they really were, not just for what they felt like. I am not dead in the earth. I am a planted seed that is very much alive and with potential that will neither be destroyed nor prematurely picked. I will bloom at the perfect time.

*****

Summer arrived in grand fashion. I looked forward to the sun, sand, clambakes and all the simple pleasures of summer at the Jersey Shore. That year, I enjoyed time with my family, especially my nieces and nephews at our shore house, though I secretly longed for Juliàn to be there. I loved to tan and swim, and my favorite thing was always to float in the pool and read. It was so relaxing, and being there was a good escape from the realities of life. It was a good summer, hot enough but not suffocating, and we spent a lot of time sunning, grilling, and enjoying the pool and shore lifestyle, though I longed to share it with him.

Sweet and sometimes not-so-sweet days of summer passed quickly as they often do. It was a workday in the end of that summer; a hot August day. You know, the kind of day that when you shut the air conditioner in the car, you feel like you cannot breathe because the sticky hot air takes over so quickly. It was the kind of day that it is a total waste to style your hair because it will either frizz out of control instantly or flatten and just lie limp in the hot humid air. It was a crime to spend it working. I should have been working on my tan.

I am not sure where we were coming from in the early afternoon, but Juliàn and I had taken a ride for something work-related for him up north. It was getting near dinnertime, and we were pretty hungry. I was feeling like we were far away from anything familiar and was not recognizing the area at all. I never liked that feeling. It was kind of like being homesick as a child. We started looking for places to stop and eat, and I spotted a cute cafe that looked cool and empty. It was actually refreshingly cold and very empty. We ordered Coke, and he smiled at me and covered both of my hands with his from across the table. Enjoying his touch, I started to cool down as we perused the menu. We ordered fried calamari, angel-hair pasta, and seafood salad. As we waited for the waitress to return, we sipped our chilled Coca-Colas, letting the sugar temporarily satisfy our hunger.

Juliàn was not himself. He was uncomfortable. I pressed him.
"What's up?"

"Nothing." He cleared his throat and smiled. It was forced.

"Any wedding plan talk?" I knew she was planning. I knew it. I just had not heard it yet.

"She says September 3, but I don' tink—" He let it slip out, but I abruptly cut him off.

"WHAT? You picked a date? Were you going to tell me?"

"I didn't pick nuting…she say September twentieth or thirtieth. I don' really care at all wha' she does. Let her plan."

The lump came, and I felt pins and needles slowly climb up my spine. I excused myself. Streaming tears rolled down my face. I slapped my cheeks looking in the mirror and washed my face to stop it. I was not crying *for* her or him anymore. I was going to march back, eat my dinner, and enjoy the night, and that is just what I did.

Later that night, my courage faded and I cried myself to sleep. I wondered how and when this would ever end. Thoughts of suicide ran through my clouded head. I thought about different methods— sure, if I took a lot of pills, it would all be over. I knew what would work. I knew how not to make a mistake and not wake up a vegetable. My strength was gone. I was broken. The downward spiral had really begun.

Chapter 28

Loyal Friends and Self-Worth

I am a good friend. I am the friend anyone can call on for help, especially in a time of crisis. I have a very sympathetic ear and a heart to help, especially when it comes to a relationship problem. I am clear to communicate my thoughts after hearing about a situation because I am a good listener, and I pay attention. More than that, I actually do care. I feel grateful that my advice has helped my friends and others in various situations over the years. It is truly gratifying to help someone in need and witness the resolution of the problem after seeing and feeling the pain of it. I have always been a loyal friend, and with most, we have remained friends for many years. These people are the kind of friends who I can be apart from for a very long time and then when we are together, we pick up where we left off. Sometimes with these friends, we can pick up the conversation started a month or a year or two ago, as if there was no time in between. True friendship is priceless. The older I become, the more I realize that people can be really disappointing and how precious the friends who never disappoint really are. I am grateful for the good friends in my life, because they really are few and far between.

It is ironic when people disappear from your everyday life for a long time—maybe even forget you are alive—until they need something. My friends know that my confidence in the goodness of God is a driving force that enables me to help. I have strong opinions and present them as just that—opinions—but I never judge and I would drop anything to come running to help. My problem was if I needed the same help, asking for and receiving it was very difficult for me. You cannot be a teacher before you are a student. You cannot be a mentor before you are mentored, and you cannot continually give and not receive. In fact, if we do not maintain that healthy balance, our lives begin to get off-kilter, and things begin to go awry. Something inside suffers if you are always giving and not receiving. It is okay to receive. It is okay to be vulnerable. It is okay to occasionally be the center of attention. It is a good thing to be treated well by others. We hear and sometimes listen to voices inside from negative experiences in our past that feed our doubts about self-worth. They try to make us believe we are less than who we really are. We must tune those voices out and erase those negative thoughts by replacing them with positive ones. My strategy has been to feel a negative feeling or think a negative thought, but then I say out loud the opposite, even if was not true at the time. For instance, if I am feeling ugly and my mind is telling me I am ugly and a loser, I say out loud, *"I am beautiful and loveable. I am a winner. I am attractive. People love me, and I love them back."* This is such a simple thing to do, but it has the potential to completely change a situation and our lives. It is an effective strategy to use daily. Your mind has no choice but to listen if you are talking out loud. The outside sounds drown out the inside thoughts. This is how you can change your negative thoughts. It is a process and your passion and your persistence to this concept determines how soon you will be free of negative thinking, or at least to be able to manage it and shut the negative off.

Blessed—being in a desirable state, having more than you need, being in a state of receiving good and being able to give. I do not see that as being spoiled but rather being preserved! Each person's "desirable state" is personally defined. Living in a desirable state and being content is certainly what was intended for us all. This is a concept to embrace, not to be embarrassed of. It is something to seek to be and to have. It starts with self-awareness—the awareness of our own strengths and weaknesses, the awareness of our possibilities and limitations, and the awareness of a gracious God, Who desires to pour out on us if we would only let Him.

*****

Time was moving faster than I realized. I made it through the winter and another cycle of ups and downs. The downs kept getting lower. Emotional lows were causing deep wounds, and the recoveries for me were slower and longer leaving me with partially healed wounds that were more vulnerable to migrant emotional infectious diseases. Every incident was taking more and more from me. I felt as though I was being erased from the inside out.

It was springtime, a time for change. Time for fresh air and more welcoming temperatures. Spring is a time for newness and growth, but this year, nothing was fresh for me. Spring is the time when you can hang your washed clothes outside to dry in the warm sunlight, smelling so fresh from the fabric softener they were rinsed in. I felt like old, dirty clothes stuck in the same old hamper. More and more infrequently, I got a whiff of freshness, but that was a quickly passing sensation in my life. I always seemed to end up back in the dirty laundry, wondering how I got there and why I could not seem to get out. I was suffocating under that soiled, stinky pile of used clothes.

"Did she pick a time and place to get married? Is it definitely September?" We were sitting in the car after lunch, as usual.

"No, no, no, no, no, no! I tol' her we just engaged. We not gonna plan nuthing."

I did not totally buy it, but something inside me had to believe he would never go through with it. He claimed he gave her a ring to shut her up and calm her down, and I chose to believe him. I told myself it was not really a lie if we both believed it, and I did not want to hear any advice from anyone else. He just needed time. I pictured the moment it would end completely for them. Him telling her he is through and leaving her at the altar. What a statement he would make for me! I believed it with all my heart, though the nights got longer and the days more difficult. It was becoming hard for me to do anything at all.

Chapter 29

The Pain Is So Deep

I could not get out of bed. It was too hard. Something prevented me from sitting up and getting ready, like gravity on steroids, pulling me into my mattress forcing me to close my eyes and sleep.

How did I get here? How do I get out? The phone rang, startling me out of my thoughts, reminding me that I had responsibilities. I had to shower. I had no choice. I had to fake-live through another day until I could go home and go to sleep again.

The warm shower water hit me like tiny pins. They felt stimulating at first and then they hurt. They felt like tiny, pulsating daggers soliciting the tears from my eyes that had become part of my daily routine. I heard my own whining and sobbing, and it disgusted me but I could not make it stop. I could barely stand in the shower. My head and body had no strength but to lean on the tiled wall. I was broken.

I stepped out of the shower too tired to get dressed. I knew I had patients to see and care for. I had a responsibility to diagnose and treat and do anything in my power to help them get better. I was the one to hear their complaints and address them. Sometimes just a hello and light conversation to show I cared when checking in on them was enough. *Just get dressed,* I told myself. I dressed and started my car. Driving up the Garden State Parkway lost in my hopeless thoughts, the tears returned with a vengeance. I tried to shake it, but

I could not. *Please stop, please stop, please stop.* My head was screaming, *You're stronger than this. You're not alone. You're okay! You can beat this sadness, you know how. Think about your amazing father and family and friends. Think about your patients and how sick and sad and poor and lost so many are. STOP IT! You are blessed. Focus. FOCUS. Just think about your boss and how you need to work!* But I could not stop crying. The tears came like an avalanche, rolling down my face in an icy, hot fury stinging my cheeks, shrinking my eyes. I had to pull over. I could not see. Cars were racing past me as I sat on the shoulder of one of the busiest thoroughfares in New Jersey. Thoughts of suicide again came to mind. I didn't want to hurt my dad, but I was hurting him this way too. I was sure I had become an embarrassment to him. How did I get here?

The phone rang again. It was Lorenzo. I guess his inner radar was alerting him. He seemed to always call when I cried. Well, not always. It was always my dad who called when I was crying (which was way too often). Sitting alone and crying had become a normal part of my life. It would come on me suddenly most times, like a speeding train passing a station it wasn't stopping at. I had to surrender most times. It had the power of that train too. Lorenzo was calling, but I couldn't answer the phone. I couldn't speak. I was too emotional and my voice was so tired. I heard his voice mail. *"Hey sis... You okay? Just calling to say I love you. You are special. You are amazing. Call me, I want to talk to you."* While I was listening to this, he called again and again. His radar was off the hook. He had called me like that so many times, relentlessly in pursuit, like a bloodhound who picked up a scent, and he was stubborn. He would not take no for an answer unless I matched his strength, which under the circumstances was not likely. Sometimes he called while I was sitting in my car crying my eyes out in the nearby park or any city street. When that sadness overwhelmed me, it drained my energy like a helium balloon with a leak falling from the air and hitting the ground. Sometimes he called when I was slumped over at my desk in desolation. Inevitably it was my dad or Lorenzo every time. They knew instinctively when I was sitting on the side of the road, powerless, and they both had enough of seeing me suffer. This time it was Lorenzo, and he was not going to stop calling. I knew it as he texted in between the calls. Desperate for the ringing to stop, I answered, and he knew immediately that my voice was altered.

"Hey! I have been calling you. What is wrong? I know something is not good... You are crying, neh? Enough! Sis! You have cried enough tears to fill an ocean. Enough! Where are you? I am coming," he insisted.

I answered, *"Thanks, but I am okay."*

Lorenzo was not buying it. *"NO sis! No! You are not okay! You are better than this! From now on you stay in my house after work. You sleep here if you need to. When you are home, if you cannot get out of bed, I will come and wake you. After work, you come to my house. I will not take no for an answer. You do not need to be alone. You stay here, in my house as long as you have to. This is over!"*

He was right and I had no strength to resist, so I agreed. But it wasn't the end. It was just the beginning.

Chapter 30

Feelings

I have explained to people for a lot of years the difference between feeling a certain emotion and being moved by it. Feelings come and go. They change by the minute, sometimes by seconds. If we acted on every feeling we have all the time, most of us would either end up dead or in jail. The merry-go-round of emotions will spin us out of control fast. Of course we feel, but with some feelings, we must feel them and not act upon them. We must not be always moved by how we feel.

In the hustle and bustle of every day, I often feel like punching people in the face. If you happen to live in the Northeast in the USA, you understand this well! You know, like when for no good reason someone jumps in front of me in the line at the grocery store and acts like they were there already? I feel like ramming my car into the back end of the small, old car that cuts me off and then brakes. If I act on these feelings, the consequences will be much more severe than if I just feel the feeling of anger and let it pass.

This is true with feelings of rejection and emotional pain as well. We feel the pain so deeply and strongly that it attempts to incapacitate us. We must get up and out of bed and go to work. We must realize that rejection could be the hand of God protecting us. We must not see ourselves as rejected but protected. We must resist the labels life and situations try to permanently place on us: *reject, hurt, lonely, damaged*. In resisting the labels, we resist believing in them and then we cannot be moved by them! We limit the power of those labels. I am not a loser because I lose sometimes. I am not helpless because sometimes I need help. I am not damaged because I have weathered a terrible life storm.

Feelings—fleeting sensations about circumstances in our lives are not always the truth of the matter. For instance, if a relative is coming to visit on a plane, we feel excited. We prepare for their arrival, and we feel anticipation and excitement. We drive halfway to the airport and hear that the flight is delayed five hours. We may feel angry and disappointed and even some fear that they may never get here, but that does not change the truth that the plane is in the sky and arriving soon. It doesn't change the initial feeling of happiness to see that person. The anger and disappointment is fleeting. It is temporary. Temporary situations, especially negative ones that seem to have the power to destroy, do not define us if we do not let them. The fact is, we feel strong feelings for real reasons. The truth is they do *not* define us. As my daddy taught me, truth overrides fact.

We feel strong feelings, but we cannot be moved by them. If we feel the feeling but do not act, it will pass, and the truth will prevail.

*****

It was a beautiful Saturday morning. I was with him all week, and I knew this day was coming. I had not really slept much at all that week. Why should I? How could I? The man who promised me the world, who I was helplessly in love with, and who I believed was my husband-to-be was marrying someone else. Was I *really* this person? Did I *really* let this happen? What world had I created? Would I ever get out of it? If so, how?

I kept fantasizing that he would leave her at the altar and appear at my door, breathless and passionate, dressed in a tuxedo with an untied tie, grabbing me close, telling me he loved me, and whisking me away somewhere, like a good romantic movie. I kept hoping and hoping this was not just a fantasy. I even thought about getting dressed and packing a bag—ready to open the door, ready to escape, together in love, holding each other tightly.

I felt embarrassed as I recalled the many promises he made to me that I believed. How could I possibly believe things like, *"We will be together, baby, even if we separate for a little while. You are the one for me. I will come back for you! I promise. This is temporary. I tol' you I owe her. You will see and if you are with someone else, you will leave him when I come back for you..."*

There are many counselors, psychologists, preachers, and every day ordinary people who will offer reasons for why I let something like this happen to me. As a matter of fact, I used to be one of them. The idea of walking in another person's shoes is a profound concept that we should give deep consideration to. When the rubber meets the road at crisis times in our lives, we desperately need someone to overlook the mistakes and not judge the terribly poor decisions we have made. We need someone to offer a long, long rope of love and grace into the deep hole of guilt and shame and desperation we are sinking into so that we can grab it, hold on, and pull ourselves up, never letting go, because it is saving our life. I did not know this then. I stayed cooped up home in front of my computer, searching wedding venues they might have been at. I answered everyone (except my father and Juliàn) by texts all day, explaining that I was sick with no voice and a fever, which actually was true. I had no voice, no strength, no will to exist. The sobbing, depression, lack of sleep and desperation to die made it all worse. The day was so bright, but I felt so dark and heavy. I think maybe for the first time in a long time Juliàn was afraid I might do something crazy like show up and scream or cause a ruckus or even worse. I had been acting a little crazy, and why wouldn't I? I was in a ludicrous, beyond ridiculous situation. I was a strong person of faith with a supportive family and a very successful career, but I was in a predicament that was draining the life out of me. Not just draining the life out of me but robbing me of every moment. It could make a person do a lot of dumb things. I am sure his fear of me snapping prevented him from telling me exact times or locations for this joyous event.

All I had was the Internet and Ian's Facebook page, which I checked as often as possible between crying my eyes out on my floor in front of my computer. My day was split between looking up wedding venues I thought they could afford and sleeping and cry-ing. Once again, I clearly remember what I was wearing—an awful maroonish-colored velour pajama gown that was way too big and heavy. Its ugly color, matronly (lack of) style, and heavy dark nature fit the mourning mood I was forced into. I continued to fantasize that he would leave her groomless at the altar. I pictured him at the airport, ready to board a plane headed to the Dominican Republic, ready to call me to join him. I remember how often we talked about that very thing, plotting out several different scenarios of just how he would leave her at the altar. I pictured her alone there in her gown waiting for him then sobbing to her family. I was hopeful that she would feel just a hundredth of my pain for a change. I fell asleep to these thoughts in the middle of the afternoon. Hot and exhausted and as pale as any cartoon ghost you'd ever seen, I woke up very aware of my current situation. I jumped to check the computer and saw everything I feared. It was around five o'clock. Happy wedding pictures were posted all over Facebook. First, I saw several photos of Juliàn smiling widely in the back of a limousine alongside Ian and his groomsmen. They were laughing, and each one had a drink in his hand. Juliàn looked so handsome. I guessed they were headed to the church. Then I saw the actual wedding photos. He did not leave her at the altar at all. I saw the proof. He waited there for her at that altar, then he vowed to her, kissing her to seal it. He was not coming over any time soon. He was married. The pictures were worse than a line of shotguns pointed at me. I fell to my carpet, feeling the blood drain. I was numb and felt feverish, deep in a hole of shame and sorrow and depression, and I saw no way out. It happened. He was married. There would be no knock on my door any time soon. *He will go through these formalities and come back to me in a few months. He doesn't love her. He's being a good person and paying her back for being nice to him.* I soothed myself between the guttural sobs and I made myself believe him. It was the only way I could keep breathing.

Crying myself in and out of sleep throughout the remainder of the day and questioning why I was so dumb and so weak, I begged for the day to end. I hoped I could fall asleep and never wake up. Emotionally and physically exhausted from sobbing, I awoke to his ring tone. It was 11:40 p.m. on his wedding day. My heart really did stop for a second. Was he leaving her now to meet me? Could it be?

"*Hello?*" There was silence. "*Hello? HELLO?!*" I yelled with a raspy, tired voice with the tiniest bit of hope in it. But no one replied. I sat up fast in my bed in complete darkness, so fast I got very light-headed. What happened was worse than I could have imagined. Somehow (probably because he was in a drunken stupor) his phone had dialed me. For the next twenty minutes I heard him asking his friends and family if they had enough to drink. I listened intently to mumbled Dominican Spanish that I could only partially understand mixed with giggling and laughing. I heard him being his gentle self, speaking graciously to his friends and family. Then I heard her loud and obnoxious voice. It cut through me like a chef's-grade steak knife cuts through soft butter. I could feel the wound from it begin to bleed inside the deepest part of my gut. She was thanking the family in a semiformal speech. She was so nauseating. She begged to be the center of attention. So opposite of me, she reveled in it, and I loathed it. It was the end of a perfect day for the happy couple, and I got to hear it firsthand. I could have stayed on the phone. I could have listened more. What was the point? I hung up and cried myself back to sleep once again, hoping I would never wake up.

Ian was the first one to call me in the morning. He seemed really concerned about me. He had texted me the day before and had been saying for the last few months that he did not believe Juliàn would go through with the wedding. He called me to see if I was okay, and he reassured me that he and Juliàn were with their friends the entire reception and that he married her out of obligation and that Juliàn really loves me. He told me to relax and be calm. He told me this did not mean anything, that Juliàn was trapped and just keeping his word. I believed him, and I think he believed what he said too. Although I think that was my way to cope, I knew Juliàn was simply too weak to fight her. She was strong and controlling. I had witnessed it many times, and I knew his personality well. Within a few minutes, he called, interrupting my thoughts. It is very, very difficult to write how I felt, but I will try. His voice was very low and the pace was very slow and calm. He spoke softly, and he cleared his throat a lot. He sounded distant, but he felt nearby, and he was calling me baby. I could not decide if he was bothered by me, afraid of me, really sad for me, or just missing me. Maybe it was a combination of emotions, but it was strange. I felt betrayed beyond belief, but incredibly, I also felt bad for him because I believed he was trapped. I felt special because he was calling me. I was on his mind. Although I was second class, he always had time for me, and he was always kind and gentle. Maybe if just once he acted like a nasty, mean jerk, I could have gotten away, but he never did, and it kept a hold on me.

He could not stay with her. He would not stay with her. He was the one for me. It was just a matter of time. I felt it. This is true love. Waiting and hoping and weathering the difficult obstacles. This is a fairy tale. I was the real princess waiting.

"So, when are you going to Mexico?" I asked. A few weeks ago, he told me that her aunt paid for a four-night honeymoon in Cancun, Mexico. I think I vomited that day, and I am sure it was a lie that the trip was a gift. They paid and they planned. I stepped out of the car and puked up my lunch. Now again today, it was just another Saturday in September for most people; but for me, everything was different. *They* were husband and wife.

"Uh, tonight," he said low, clearing his throat in between those words, then continuing, *"like aroun' seven."* He sounded so far away. Maybe he was there already. Whoever knew the truth?

"Do you feel different?" I begged.

"Wha'? No, no, no," he replied with a chuckle and another throat-clearing sound. *"I miss you. I feel so bad for you. I never meant to hurt you, baby. Are you okay? Will you be strong for me?"* he asked. Tears were streaming down my face. I do not know where they came from. I felt so dry. I do not know how I had any left to cry. I again was a waxed face melting in the heat of the moment.

"I will call as soon as I am back, okay? Nothing changed. This means nothing. I miss you."

I did not hear from him for the whole four nights and five days of his honeymoon. I went through the motions of the week, barely sleeping and picturing them making love on the beach of Cancun and in the hotel bed and hotel bathroom. In my mind, I saw them feeding each other delicacies, swimming in the clear blue ocean water by day and dancing close, whispering sweet nothings in their native language at night. I did not even exist, at least I wished I didn't. I told myself I was a fool. I told myself I would never talk to him again. I made it through a whole work week without him. I could do this. I was getting stronger every day, right? Wrong. When my phone rang his ring tone, as soon as he was back in New Jersey—married and tan and post honeymoon bliss—I answered immediately. I was sure they fought and that it was over for them. I was sure he was calling to say they were talking divorce. She got her wedding. That's what she wanted. They were unable to cohabitate. I knew it! He was mine. It was just a matter of time, just like he always said.

I had actually made it through a whole week without Juliàn. I commuted and worked and saw patients and managed my days okay. At night I watched my beautiful, exotic fish glide through my 180-gallon aquarium devouring the mini shrimp I dropped slowly into the tank. The week was over and now he was back home, back to work and soon to be back in my life. The routine began to play out again. Time was ticking, and nothing was changing. While I was crying at work almost every day and my boss began to notice, Juliàn was living the married life with her at night. My boss questioned me quite frequently about what was going on with me, and to my horror, usually all I could do was cry when I tried to answer him. I was dressing less professionally. I was wearing less makeup and jewelry, and he noticed the changes. I did my usual apology thing to him, explained I was okay, and managed to do my work. He was assured I was doing my job, but I was very sad; and I guess it was obvious because everyone noticed, but I would not let anyone in.

My father was calling me three to five times a day and texting a lot. He was and is an unbelievable pillar of strength and comfort and grace. He continued to believe and expect the best for me and was quiet and prayerful about what he knew and did not know. Sometimes I ignored his calls. I hated to do that, but it was so hard to let him hear me suffer, and it was hard to be completely truthful about the sadness in my life. He did not deserve my ignoring, but there was shame too. I never wanted to embarrass or hurt my dad. He was relentlessly calling me. He did not like me not answering, but he was very aware of my state of mind and was concerned. I tried to cover my sadness, tried to be strong on the phone, but it was very hard.

One day I was sitting at my desk at work, and he called on my private line in my office. I could tell he had something serious and special to tell me. I could tell it was encouraging and from God. You can be at your lowest point, but if you have faith, there is a flicker of hope inside no matter how desperate you feel. That flicker got a little bigger and began to shine brighter as I listened to my dad and his ever encouraging voice of hope. He explained that he had received a letter from a person who saw him preach on TV. She was from another state. She wrote him a letter, feeling prompted to tell him something. He does not know her now, did not know her then, and probably will never know her. She explained in the letter that she really enjoyed his teaching on faith and grace and how encouraging it was and how much she learned from him. She apologized before she continued, saying she knew nothing of him and his personal life but that she knew she had to tell him the next thing she said. She politely instructed my dad should do the following: *"Tell your daughter not to worry... tell her that her bread is coming home."* When my father told me about this, he asked me if it meant anything to me. I immediately thought of Juliàn and bread being representative of what we eat every day, that he was coming back to me. I told my father I had an idea of what it meant, but I asked him to explain to me what he thought, *"Well, I have three daughters, but I knew immediately it was for you, and it is about the man in your life."* As he relayed the message, he was asking over and over if I heard him and what it meant to me. Hot tears were streaming down my face before he could finish. I interpreted it as meaning what I first thought. My man was indeed coming to me, and I accepted it. I believed it. I reasoned on the inside of me, that Juliàn would leave her soon and that his wedding was never meant to be. I convinced myself that he really did marry her out of obligation and was keeping his word. It would all be okay. I trusted God with my life even though I messed it up significantly. God is a good God who cares for His own. He is gracious and full of mercy. I knew it. My husband, my bread, what I needed daily was coming home. It was just the encouragement I needed.

Chapter 31

The Worst Was Not Over

I had been struggling for months, trying to set myself free of Juliàn, but at the same time I had made myself believe that we were meant to be together. Every time I made up my mind to break free of him, something seemed to stop me. We were in a cycle of me leaving him, staying away for a few days or a week, and then creeping back. I had even helped him orchestrate leaving the company he worked for and helped him negotiate a much better job with a huge raise less than five minutes from his home. He was kind and understanding, and he continued to spend almost every day and most weekends with me. I was driving to his new job three to four times a week to meet him for lunch. I knew I was wrong, and I knew I should have given him an ultimatum and leave him until he was divorced. I had shut my right thinking down. I saw my good friends less and less. I had introduced many of them to Juliàn and to Ian too, but none of them had an interest in being with us, so we sort of became used to it being just the three of us. It worked for me.

Months had passed faster than I realized. Time was not waiting for me, and life really was passing me by. In the meanwhile, I started boxing again—well, not really boxing, but fitness training with gloves and a heavy bag that I had installed in my garage. I loved it. It was my favorite form of fitness. I had taken it up a few years earlier to kickstart weight loss and had success with it.

One day, I came home from work, speaking to Juliàn on the phone. He was going to the gym with Ian, and I was going to punch the heavy bag that was hanging in my garage. I was pretty good at it, and I really liked the results I was getting and the way it made me feel. That particular day, I had been feeling really good. Work went well, I had lunch with Juliàn, and the weather was delightful. I had not punched in quite a while, but it was spring, and I felt motivated. It was my father's birthday, and my plan was to work out hard then go have dinner with him.

I changed my clothes and punched for almost an hour. I felt tired but invigorated. I felt motivated. I felt alive again, better than I had for a long time. I called my father to tell him my plan to go see him, and I even said to him, *"Dad, my hair is growing again!"* I like to talk like that with my dad. You know, using scripture references vaguely. He always gets it immediately. I was referring to Samson gaining his strength back by letting his hair grow and heading for the biggest victory of his life. *"I punched for almost an hour! I feel so great!"*

My father chuckled and mumbled, *"Good, honey,"* happy for me and understanding me perfectly. He congratulated me for a moment, and I hung up the phone. He was chuckling with pride. At the same time I was on the phone with my dad, I was perusing through Facebook on the computer. What I saw in the next few moments nearly killed me. I am not being dramatic. If it were not for the grace of God, I do not think I would have made it. I was sure I had endured the worst—an engagement, a wedding, a romantic honeymoon, all with persistent, pervasive promising that I was the one and all the rest was temporary and meant nothing. But I was completely unprepared for this. The possibility never ever crossed my mind. Call me an idiot. It was a post by *her*—a hand drawn picture of a twelve-week-old fetus complete with an explanation. My baby is now three months. It has eyes and toes and... *We* cannot wait to meet you!

I clutched my chest. My legs got weak. My heart was pounding out of control. I was shaking so hard. I dialed my father back out of instinct. I was dying. I was sure I would die. He picked up immediately, but I could not speak. Nothing would come out.

"Hello? HELLO? Cynthia? CYN? Are you okay? CYNTHIA?" My father was nearly screaming, stricken with fear and frantic because I am sure all he heard coming from me were gasps for air. He knew I had just done a tough workout. I am sure he was really worried. I hated myself for putting him through this, but I could not speak.

My body was trembling so hard, I thought I would break apart and crumble. After minutes, I finally pushed something out, *"She... sheee...shee'sssss...she'sss...pre...preggg....prrregnant!"*

"I'll be right over. DON'T DO ANYTHING! Cyn! Cynthia? CYNTHIA ANNE?!" But I had already hung up and started to dial Juliàn in a spinning, seething rage.

"LIAR! You lying animal! I hate you! I HATE YOU! SHE'S PREGNANT?? SHE'S PREGNANT?? I hate you, and I hate her. I hate you, you disgusting, heartless, liar...I HAAATE YOUUUUUU!" I was screaming and shaking so loud and so hard. My throat was on fire, my body a trembling inferno of rage. *"How could you do this to me? HOW COULD YOU DO THIS? Don't you ever, EVER talk to me again, you lying worthless trash!"* My voice and strength were gone. I could feel life and the desire to live draining from me. I collapsed backward onto my couch, gazing at the ceiling, gasping for air. My phone kept ringing and ringing. I could feel the deep sobs stirring inside about to bubble up and pour out. And when they did, I screamed and sobbed and paced and panted like a rabid animal. My mind stopped working.

I saw that Ian was calling, so I picked up to scream at someone, but I could barely talk. *"What happened, Cynthia? All of a sudden, Juliàn started crying so hard and so bad. He ran out of the gym, and I can't find him. What did you say to him? I am so worried about him... and you! What's going on, sweetie?"*

"Shut up, Ian. I hate you too, Ian! As if you don't know, you lying fake!" I was so mad, so devastated, but he was lost. He had no clue what was happening. He knew something was really bad, and he would not stop asking what happened. *"Sweetie, please calm down and tell me what happened. I don't understand."*

"She's pregnant?! PREGNANT?! You don't know?" It took a few minutes of me listening to him and his sheer surprise. He did not know. In fact, he had no idea; and the fact that his best friend, his compadre,

his confidant knew nothing, comforted me for a fleeting moment. It made me think that Juliàn was desperately trying to figure out what to do. He was genuinely confused. I *had* to believe that to survive.

"*Whaaaaaaaat? Who? Wait...WHAT are you talking about?*" Ian had to think to put it all together. He was shocked and upset. "*Oh my God. I didn't know. I swear to God I didn't know, honey. Please calm down. It's gonna be okay. Please calm down.*" My father walked in and took the phone.

"*Ian, this is Cynthia's father. What's going on? Where is Juliàn?*" And he said a lot of *uh huhs* and *mm-hmms* and then hung up. I was spinning, sweating, panting.

My father explained that Ian was really concerned about Juliàn, who had fled the gym crying a lot. He was calling and calling, but Juliàn wouldn't answer. I was a little worried. I remember the darkness and the pain and the disbelief. Like when a close relative dies. You just cannot believe it—SHOCK. But this was not death—it was a new life that he made with *her*.

My father called Juliàn and being the amazing man that he is, realized how much pain he was in. Juliàn kept apologizing and crying and threatening that he just wanted to die, and my dad talked him down from the ledge. He begged to talk to me, but I shook my head to my dad. He swore he was not going home that night. He swore to my dad that he made a mistake, that she trapped him because he wanted to leave her. It was all so desperate, so pathetic, so unbelievable. He even said he secretly hoped it was not true and followed that with tears and guilty sobs. It was a desperate situation all around, and it warranted the faith and love of my daddy, and the grace of my God.

I cannot make you feel the pain of that day or the week or the month or that year. It is the love and faith of my father that got me through—for sure. My father was saying he was going to take me to the hospital. He was very concerned saying he never saw me that way and that I needed help. I resisted, but I was pretty far gone. I feared that I might never be totally coherent and normal again. I just wanted to die so bad, SOOO BAD, but I didn't. Sheer exhaustion let me fall asleep. I slept and slept and slept.

For the next week, my father and Lisa from Ohio, nursed me back to an emotional crawl. I still just wanted to die. There was no other choice. I took a week off work to stay in my bed. It did not matter whether he had "made a mistake," as he said or not. He did not even have the guts to tell me, and I am not sure which was worse. I laid in bed day and night, talking only to Lisa and my dad. We reasoned that children never really stop true love, and if it was meant to be, this would not stop it. Those conversations gave me hope for where I was at, and one month later, for the first time, I wrote what I was feeling, still trying to convince myself it was all okay. For the first time, I sat in my kitchen and wrote how I felt:

Does the pain ever stop? Will my broken heart ever mend? The loss is palpable, disconcerting, and thick. Like food that is lukewarm and flat and doesn't want to go down. The change is here. It's clear. It's different. He is different—his voice, his words. I can feel his life going forward while mine slowly dissolves, losing the zest and oomph it had with him in it, like Coca-Cola that sat on the counter too long. Will the pain and longing stop? Will he ever look me in the eye again? The sadness is sitting on my chest like humidity in the summer in New York City. I hear my rapid breathing when I think about all the dreams—gone. I bite my lip and wipe my eyes. The intimate moments—gone. The laughing—gone. The innocence of immersing yourself in something so delicious—gone. The feeling that dreams can come true and the future together is sooo hopeful—gone. My steps are so heavy like my pockets are full of wet rocks, my eyes hard to open. All I want is a phone call that lets me know he thinks of me, but I know the time span between each call is growing like the life he made inside of her.

In the next few months, I became completely unraveled. I hit rock bottom. I started planning the end of my life, picturing the best way to die and hoping my father would be okay with it. It was now just a matter of when. I knew how.

Chapter 32

Hurricane Irene

By summer I was feeling every bad emotion a person possibly can. He was seeing me a lot less but calling more. He was 'stuck' with her more and more. A hurricane, Irene, was predicted and came. There was terrible flooding all over New Jersey. He had to stay home with her and be close to work. Her car broke down for the last time, and they shared his while shopping for a new one. I began to resent his weakness. I began to believe that he really was stuck with a woman who controlled him. I wrote my sarcastic and angry feelings down again.

> *The whole weekend with her. Friday afternoon, Friday night, Saturday, Saturday night, all day Sunday, Sunday night. You can't even drive anywhere alone. Everything is together now. "Esposos para siempre…" That's what she wrote one time to you on a social page. I saw it. You ignored her comment. So mean to her. I feel sorry for her, but not really. She is a terrible person too. She planned to clip your wings, stop you from flying. She put that on a public page too, and you laughed and shook your head. She married you "even if you get divorced in a week." You owed her, my God, what a pathetic pair.*

You have everything together, one year of marriage. You don't even see your friends anymore.

She wins. She clipped your wings and got control of you. She said she would with an evil, taunting, laugh, and you said, "NEVER." But she did, and she got EVERYTHING she wanted. You got her. Just like she planned. "Hahahaha" is what she thinks…And "Let me die" is what I think. Nope, I will not die. Instead, I will face it. It is time for me to set you free. I have to let go. The hole inside has ripped me apart. It is time for me to get put back together. It is time for me to let you be. I am not sure where I will go or what I will do. Not sure if I can go on. But I have to move away. You believe she needs you, and I don't. Couldn't you have said that a year ago? You say you don't even like her family. You say you don't get along. You tell me to be patient. I cannot afford to buy the lies anymore. You swore you loved me. You swore you would leave her. The lies have bankrupted my soul. I am lost. I am sad. I am alone. Your life is full of happiness. Mine is so empty, so sad. Yours is full of new. Together. You try to hide it all. You love your life. You are having a baby— together! Happy anniversary! I am celebrating the pain over and over. I am drifting…afloat on a sea of pain and sadness. Existing. Drifting…

Let me go. Do not feel bad for me. I chose this. Over and over and over. So dumb.

You cannot take this? You cannot handle it? This is no longer about you.

*****

177

I woke up sobbing again. It seemed impossible that it could be worse than previous times. But it was. I was sleeping less and less. I had no strength and no motivation, and I felt like I was losing my mind. I thought of getting in my car and driving until I was thousands of miles away. I thought of flying to an island to vacation but really to be isolated and lie down and die and never come back to sadness. In fact, I had been researching exotic vacation spots to go away again for weight loss and isolation and exercise, but nothing ever worked out at all. I showered and put on sweats. What started out as aimless turned in to a decisive plan. I drove to the new clinic he worked in, the one I helped him get hired in. The one I coached him through the application process and interview. The one I helped him get for almost double what he was making. I drove like I was drunk. I was a mess. Undone. Unraveled.

I parked my car inconspicuously, shut the engine off, opened all the windows, and moved my seat back. The sun was hot, and a hot wind was blowing. It was unlike me to just sit and feel hot, but I was not me at all, and I did not know who I was becoming. He told me for months and months—years now—that she meant nothing to him, that he was with her because he couldn't be a jerk. She was eight months pregnant with his baby. I knew it was a girl, and I even knew her name. I knew her due date. He told me everything. I watched his white car pull up. She was driving. He jumped out laughing and chatting with four Dunkin' Donut cups in hand to bring inside. He never had time to get me coffee! I always had to stop and get it and pay for it. He walked to her side of the car, the driver's side, kissed her fast but easily, and went inside. I saw her swollen belly and smiling face as she pulled away. Crying uncontrollably, I called him immediately from my car.

"*Get out here, you liar. I saw you. I saw the happy couple kiss goodbye. I saw the coffee you brought everyone but can never bring me.*"

"*Wha? Was wrong wit' you? Where are you? You are here now? Oh my God. You' crazy. I'm tired of this. I cannot come now. Jus' wait a few minutes.*"

"*What? You're tired of this?* YOU'RE TIRED?" I was screaming, but he had hung up. I looked and thought and felt like a crazy person. I was crying uncontrollably with no makeup and messy hair, sitting in a parked car with open windows in ninety-degree heat. My seat was reclined so far back it was almost flat. I felt a little afraid. I felt like I lost it. When I say "crying uncontrollably," I mean it. Deep, long, breath-stealing sobs were coming from way down deep inside of me, and they wouldn't stop.

Suddenly, completely out of nowhere, the wind picked up, and the car began to rock side to side, rhythmically, fast. For a few seconds, I thought I was in a dream. It was surreal. It stopped my sobbing and gave me the strength to sit up. I was petrified as I watched piles of dirt moving in fast circles in the unfinished section of the new parking lot. And then suddenly again, just like it started, the wind and shaking stopped.

I fell back into my seat. What on earth just happened?

There were people starting to file out of the medical building. What was this? What was happening? As I watched the building empty as people continued to exit and congregate outside, I turned on the radio to find out that northern New Jersey had experienced an earthquake. This rare earthquake measured 5.8 on the Richter scale. What a metaphor. It was time for an earthquake in my life to shake it up and rock me back to my senses!

Eventually, Juliàn was able to come out to the car, but nothing was done or said that mattered at all. We were both only talking about and thinking about the earthquake. He was chattering on and on about this record-breaking event in New Jersey. He always managed to avoid really talking about us. I was thinking about my own personal earthquake. I went home as exhausted and sad and tired as ever, but I was definitely shaken.

Chapter 33

Minas Gerais Is
Not the Answer

PJ had begun selling motorcycles in a very busy store in Middlesex County, and he was doing really well. He was talking to Josianne every day, and she was telling him how she missed him and how she wanted him to return to Minas soon. He assured her that he would return soon, and every day he hung up the phone happy, contemplating the next trip, but secretly missing something; he just was unsure of what. He was holding his own in sales and even made 'top salesman of the month' more than a few times.

About two months after being back in New Jersey, PJ settled into his life of selling bikes six days a week, talking to Josianne on the phone daily, and spending Sundays with his son. The routine calls to Brazil usually had Josianne answering and talking about everything they could. One routine day of the week, PJ called Josianne, and her mother answered the phone. Hearing uneasiness in her voice, he immediately asked if everything was okay. PJ listened closely as her mother explained that she could not be dishonest with him because he was so good and kind to her daughter. With a soft and somewhat broken voice, she explained that she had been crying all morning because earlier that day, Josianne had packed her bags in a huff and left the house with another man.

Confused and broken, with little to say, PJ thanked her mother for her honesty, wished her the best, hung up the phone, and realized this same pain was happening to him again. Although he never questioned God, he wondered what he was doing wrong to elicit this painful pattern. He wondered if his dreams of love and stability would ever come true. He longed to be loved like he loved. He wanted a stable family life at home, and although he was good at sales and incredibly successful there, he sensed a greater purpose for his life. For now, he would love his son and put his hand to the plow, numbed by the sting of this rejection, but refusing to let it get the best of him.

Chapter 34

Dreams of Success

Dreams of success are natural in all of us. It is our destiny to succeed. We hope and plan and watch failures from afar and secretly say, "That will never be me." But no amount of planning can stop an out-of-control freight train as it leaps off the track heading toward you. If you cannot get out of its way, it will knock you down, flatten you out, and paralyze you. Without a lot of intervention, it will kill you.

*****

After a few more apologies, promises and laughs, Juliàn and I were again eating lunch in the parking lots of different centers and actually going to restaurants. It had only been a few weeks since the earthquake, and on this day, we were in the parking lot of a different center than usual. *She* had called to warn him to stay close to where they lived. Her doctor had advised she would go into labor in the next few days. He left a few minutes after that call, and I tried to have a normal afternoon. I was planning my permanent departure from him and desperately trying to muster up the strength to walk.

I had a dinner scheduled for patients later that day, and I was very preoccupied during it. People were laughing, eating, and enjoying our generosity during that patient education dinner. They were thanking me and chatting, and I was trying so hard to be engaging and concerned like usual, but I was in another place. I was waiting and watching my phone like a hawk for the call. It did not come. The anticipation robbed me of my sleep that night and the next three. The inevitable call came two days later. It was a Friday at around 5:00 p.m. He said he was going to the hospital and he would call me as soon as he could to keep me posted. I told myself she was a surrogate for me. I rehearsed that he had one more thing to go through with her and then he would leave her. Somehow, I was calm. In my disillusioned state, with his dead-in-the-eye promises and constant complaints about her and life with her, I had to believe he was the one for me and that this was all a distraction.

I went on Facebook a few hours later, and there was the picture of the baby, bundled and new, with a loving welcome message from a cousin and a whole lot of Facebook "likes" and "congratulations" comments. I fell apart. I cried so hard and so loud that I pretty much passed out on my couch. Two hours later, the phone rang. Startled from my sleeping, I answered with a tired, raspy hello. Juliàn was so excited. I congratulated him and told him to go be with them. He said he was fine to talk. He asked if I was okay. He said one day we would experience this together because he could not explain how it feels, and I needed to experience it. He sounded so sincere, but I just wanted to sleep, so I said good-night, and that's what I did.

Two days passed. My dad was calling three to four times a day as well as texting to be sure I was okay. I put up a good front, but I was at the end of my rope. I had become the girl I swore I would never ever be. I was reduced to groveling. Juliàn was married with a baby, and for a while, I actually was disillusioned enough to believe that baby would be mine and we would raise it together. I did. I let go of every bit of dignity and sense I had.

Juliàn begged for me to come and see him. In the third day of his baby's life, I drove an hour up the Garden State Parkway to the hospital where *she* delivered her baby. I picked him up there on a gloomy autumn night in the front of that medical center to buy him dinner while she waited for him inside with her new infant. I was delusional. I do not even think I was desperate. I was blinded by the kindness that always seemed to flow freely from his silver-lined tongue and the belief that he loved me as much as I loved him and that he was dealing with his own demons too. We could weather this superstorm.

We drove around a lot, trying to pick a restaurant. We picked a terrible one—one step above fast food. It was greasy, loud, and crowded, and I hated it almost as much as I hated myself. The place did not matter; I could not eat. I pretended to be happy, but I was a wreck inside. He had a plastic hospital bracelet on, identifying him as the father. The baby's name was on it. I felt a little sicker every time I saw it, so I made a mental note not to look at his wrist. I looked up at his face, more than ready to get out of there. He was glowing. I was a fraud. I was a liar. What was I doing here? I wanted out.

"Let's get the check," I said.

"You okay? I mean, are you okay wit' everyt'ing? We are okay?" he probed.

"Yep! Happy for you." I tried my best to pretend, and he bought it. I think he just didn't care. He had everything. He held me in the car and tried for a few minutes to make me forget. But the blaring reality would never go away. His child had arrived and was here to stay.

He kissed me good-night, told me he would call me in a little while and got out of the car in front of the hospital. I watched him walk back inside. He even turned around and waved to me, unafraid that anyone could be watching. I felt dead inside. Numb. I felt every terrible emotion one could feel: guilt, shame, anger, disappointment, fear, betrayal, and deceit. I actually even felt happy for him and a new life. I could go on and on with how I thought and what I felt about me, until suddenly I started thinking about *him.* Who does what he just did? Who kisses his wife that just gave birth and his new baby in the hospital, steps outside, and gets picked up by his girlfriend that he swears he is totally in love with and is planning to leave his wife for to go to dinner to celebrate? Did he love me that much or was he a coldhearted person with no interest in anyone but himself? Was this worth holding on to? Was I really reduced to this, and would I continue in this awful pattern?

Arriving home after a soul-searching ride back down the Parkway, I could barely get into my bed. I felt anxious and irritated. This was a serious crossroad. Did I really want to be this person? Restless, I decided to look on Facebook again and look clearly at everything I tried so hard to believe did not exist, like the *love* between them or the fact that they were a happy family even though he strayed often. All I saw were pictures, happy comments, congratulations, and loving words from *her* to him. Just further proof of the truth. If I did not do something very soon, I surely would trade my successful destiny for much less than zero, and that just was not the stock I was made of. It was mid-October. Soon, a new season would begin.

Chapter 35

The Refinery

Diamonds are the hardest natural substance known to man. They are found in igneous rock and are essentially composed of a chain of atoms of carbon that have crystallized. This type of crystallized rock takes thousands of years to form on the earth's crust as a result of volcanic action. In order for this rudimentary rock to form a diamond, it goes through an extremely complex process, and it takes a specific set of circumstances to become refined and precious.

I grew up believing in the power of faith and believing and speaking what I wanted even if it did not seem possible. I still do. These principles were established by God, and they work. The thing is, I mistakenly believed that I would not have to experience adversity or challenges if I was constantly in a state of faith and trusting. I thought I would never have to go through trials—especially major trials. I could just use my faith to avoid them or, at worst, overcome them very quickly. I was sorely mistaken.

God does not bring adversity to us. He does not test us with problems. He is the one who equips us to not only face a challenge but to overcome it. There are always lessons to be learned and terrible side effects to avoid. Because God sees all we go through, and because He is good, He takes what is meant for our harm and uses it for our good. His grace preserves us from being damaged as we go through the storms of life while He protects and supports us. They can actually make us better, stronger, and well able to weather the next things that come against us.

Like the hardest and most valuable substance on earth, we too must go through an extensive process. You see, we all have what it takes to become a diamond. Without the refining process, we will never shine. Do not fight the process—go through it in faith, trusting in God's goodness. I promise, you will come out refined and shining brilliantly.

*****

People will walk into your life at the right time for the right reasons. Sometimes the wrong people come at the right time too, and because of this, we get confused and resist the love and intervention from the right people. Thankfully, the right people appeared for me again—at the right time and for the right reasons. Boy, am I glad I let it happen. I am forever grateful for them.

I had become close to a beautiful, kind pharmaceutical representative named Lisa. She would pop in to sell us medicine for our patients and bring lunch for us to enjoy while explaining how to prescribe the drug, how it works, and who to use it on. After business and dessert, we would chat about life and love and whatever else we could until we had to get back to work. Since an hour every few months at work doing business was not really enough time to talk and share our lives, we began talking on the phone and had become friends. I told her about Juliàn when he and I first met because she noticed something different about me and she was sure it was "a guy." I offered her a vague description of a young, hot Latino I was "just hanging out and having fun with." We laughed about it in the beginning. In fact, she had met a younger man too and had in the last few years gotten engaged and married to him.

Lisa was also a NJ Italian who had a truly professional presence for work but was tough and confrontive and honest in life. She had a refined rawness that I loved and related to. She was always so kind and complimentary to me, and I believed her. I eventually told Lisa everything. She was very understanding and had been through a terrible marriage before. She had very unobtrusive advice and an astute listening ear. She never judged me. She believed he loved me just like Lisa from Ohio did.

One Friday in late November, I stopped by Lisa's house after work. I had done that a few times before, and that day it worked out well because her husband was working late. She was pregnant, and no one knew but me, so I loved to go there and talk about it! She had hoped and planned for the pregnancy against all odds and many disappointments, and I knew this would be it for her. I had shared my faith with her and confidently advised that she would conceive (after much frustration), and have a son, just to see and know that God was good.

Juliàn had called me while I was driving to her house, and we spoke for a while, as was the custom on Friday afternoons. He would hang up when he got home, and I wouldn't hear from him until late Saturday. It fed my depression—being alone on Friday nights and all day Saturday. Before the marriage, that had always been our time.

I parked the car and noticed the leaves blowing around in circular patterns as I was trying to end the phone call. I walked into her house with the wind as blustery and crisp as any New Jersey autumn day, and I realized he did not actually disconnect the call. At first, I tried to tell him, but he couldn't hear me; and when I tried to end the call, I couldn't disconnect either. I had no idea what was going on, so as I walked in her home, I eye-motioned to Lisa, put my phone on speaker, and pressed mute. I explained to Lisa what was going on as I sat on the couch across from her. For the next three hours, we listened to Juliàn mumbling bad Spanish to *her* while they were home with *their* baby. I heard everything including the kindness in his voice when he stopped her somewhere in *their* house to tell her, *"You know you are a great mother, right? You know that."* It was like a rusty razor on bumpy skin. Lisa and I listened to the whole family get into the car to run errands. I heard him call his friend, Juan, who I knew well from work, from his personal cell phone. I was still listening from his work phone. In Spanish that I clearly understood, I listened to him invite Juan, his friend to go to *her* mother's house for "fun" that night. I understood that Spanish perfectly, *"Shrimp, pan-*

cakes, beer, Hennessy." He had told me that he never went there, that he did not like her family at all. Everything was different now. The baby sealed the deal. They were a true family, sharing everything. *She* was obnoxiously laughing in the background. I looked at Lisa with tears rolling down my cheeks. The tears were different this time. The earthquake a few weeks before had really shaken me, and these powerful aftershocks were the final blow. God let this happen so I could see into his happy life and finally accept that he was *not* the one for me at all. He was *not* mine. He never was. He was not the bread that God promised was coming home. I knew it now. It may have taken longer than it should have, but that day, I got it. I left Lisa's house different. This cry in the car was a cleansing purge, not another pity party of despair. I felt the finality of the moment as the past year and a half of pain, frustration and sadness began to separate itself from who I truly was. The winds of change on that blustery day were blowing me back to my senses. My hair *really* was growing this time, and no Philistine and no Delilah would ever cut it off again.

Chapter 36

Turn Around

Lorenzo started calling me daily to ensure I would go to his home after work, and I did. He used to pick up the guitar spontaneously or sit at the piano and start to play, and Gabby would sing. Songs that magnified God soothed my wounded soul and ministered to me. It was like therapy, but so much better than any talking, and I never wanted it to stop. Gabby had a soft, sweet voice and a comforting spirit to match it, which balanced his confronting, assertive embrace; and when they sang together, all my pain seemed to subside. I basked in it—soaked it all in and let it wash over me like a giant surfing wave. Sometimes they sang in Portuguese—a language I knew very little about. Some of our patients at work spoke it, but I was clueless about it for the most part. I had been learning Spanish for years, pretty much teaching myself and had gotten pretty good at it. Lorenzo would always say, *"Stop with that Spanish. You need to speak Portuguese,"* and I laughed it off every time, sometimes rolling my eyes thinking, *Never.* If we pay attention and stay open, often it is the tiniest things that give us glimpses of what will come.

I had stopped by church on a Sunday morning to see my father in between services. I was still depressed and sad and was unable to get myself together to be dressed to actually be in the church service, but the worst was behind me, and I was letting go. I was a mess—something that had become normal for me. I was crying and in sweatpants, weak and sad and tired from not sleeping, but I was letting the healing process work. I planned to go away. I wanted to run off somewhere far and exotic and had been looking at destination options. I went to church to tell my father that I had to move away, that I needed a new start. I thought it would be easy to do that on a Sunday, away from the house. The minute I saw my father's kind and concerned face, I got more emotional. I called him Daddy several times, blubbering through the hurt in my heart. He started crying too. He is so sensitive and kind. I was the prodigal son, and he was there to clean me up and put his ring back on my finger. While we were in his office, I received a text from Lorenzo with sad news. They had been going through fertility treatments for a long time without success and were sure the last procedure would work. It did not. He sounded so disappointed when I called. For those few moments, I was completely focused on someone else's pain, and instinct took over. I told my dad I had to go there to comfort them, so I did. I shook myself to be strong for them. I was prepared to comfort and hold them and encourage them.

When I arrived, Lorenzo was a little sad. I hugged him and asked if he was okay. He thanked me for coming and said, *"How are you?"*

A tear escaped and trickled down. *Wow, Cynthia,* I thought. *You are so selfish.*

He told me to sit on the couch. I sat down on the couch that used to be mine, and it was so much more comfortable here. Gabby came out of her bedroom, smiling. *"Hi, Cintch,"* she said. (I secretly loved her Brazilian twist on my name.) I asked how she was. She looked great.

"Me? I'm fine, girl! Let's talk about you." Amazed at her strength, I moved slightly for her to sit. She began to talk about her life. She told me how I deserved to be loved and that what I had was not love. I heard her heartbreaking story of mistrust, betrayal, and deceptions, which she experienced years before meeting Lorenzo. I heard of how she was left not only with a ton of emotional turmoil but with a lot of debt and no more income from the betrayer, with no hope of him ever committing to her again the way she thought he once did. He had hopped on a flight five thousand miles from home with someone

else, never to return again. Until then, I did not know about this. I had no idea that she had weathered such a storm. She wanted me to hear how she had to let go of that terrible past before she was able to move forward. She shared that when she did, she was able to make a whole new life with a man who loved her the way she deserved to be loved.

Lorenzo will tell you like it is. He will make you look in his eyes. He will point his finger in your face and call you out on things. Not Gabby, she tends to be the opposite. She can be confrontational, but in general, it takes some prompting. Gabby will remain quiet, and she will guide you gently most of the time. Not that day. That day, she got in my pale, tired, swollen face and told me with wide open eyes and a clear voice that it was time to let go.

"He doesn't love you, Cintchya!" In my face, louder and louder each time and forcing eye contact, she said, *"Look at me. HE DOESN'T LOVE YOU! HE DOES NOT LOVE YOU! This is not love. He does not love you, and the sooner you see this and let him go, the sooner you will find a man who loves you like you deserve to be loved. You deserve to be loved the way you love. You deserve it."*

I was forced to swallow what she said. I believed her, but I did not want to. After all, who would? No one wants to admit they are wrong. No one wants to give in and give up on something they believed was their destiny. No one wants to believe a man they love does not love them back the same. Right in that moment, my phone rang. It was Juliàn. I answered and quickly excused myself out the door of their apartment to the hallway.

"Hello, baby. How are you?"

Baby, I thought. How ironic of him. I was sure I had asked him to stop calling me that. *"I am okay."*

"Do you want to meet me at a clinic and come for lunch?" he asked politely.

"No. I am at Lorenzo's house." I answered quickly and easily. This conversation felt strained. It was different. He was different—far away—but I was different too. I was there holding on to the threads of a blanket relationship that left me cold and alone every time. Those threads were wearing thin and were about to frazzle com-

pletely because finally, after way too long, Juliàn said what he needed to say more than a year earlier. Maybe at that time, I wasn't ready to hear it, but I was ready now. I heard him loud and clear.

"Ohhh…hahaha…Das' good, das' nice. Listen, I never meant to hurt you. I always tol' you everything. I never hid from you. But I am married and now I have a baby, and you need to experience it. Maybe someday I will give you a baby. You have to feel it. I love you, and I always will. Someday we will be together again, but not now. I don' want to hurt you anymore. I'm here for you—always—anytime. You are the most beautiful person. I hope you can be patient to wait for me. I will come back to you. I love you, and I am your friend too. I will always be here for you, and I swear to God, one day I will come back for you. Just give me some time. I want you, but I cannot come for you now."

There it was. He said it. He admitted to his life. It was like relief and disbelief ran through me together in a race to see which feeling would prevail. I chose relief as tears ran down my cheeks, slowly beginning to wash away our history. I knew at that moment I could let go completely. The process had begun, but now it would continue, and I would not go back.

Calmly, with acceptance, I responded. *"I hear you. Okay. I will let you go. I need to go back inside. I am being rude."*

"I will call you tonight to check on you," he said.

I hung up, wiped my tears, and went back inside, hoping they were singing. I was returning back to the hope, back to the healing, back to real love, and back to my senses.

Chapter 37

Thanksgiving

Thanksgiving has always been my favorite holiday. Do not get me wrong, I love Christmas. I love the hustle, the bustle, the anticipation, the lights, the wintry weather, but I love Thanksgiving a little bit more. For me, it has always represented the beginning of a new season. I am not talking about the weather. Yes, the weather is brisker and colder, and you are sure winter is coming quickly, but it is the beginning of the season for giving. I love that the focus of the day is an attitude of thanks shared with family and good friends and all their quirky behaviors. Delicious smells and sounds and tastes from homemade specialties and a variety of desserts are some of the highlights of a great day that usually comes without a lot of aggravation, and it ends the same way.

The night before this Thanksgiving, I had made my demand on God. It had been a few weeks since my phone conversation with Juliàn in the hallway of Lorenzo's apartment building. We had spoken and had coffee a few times just to lessen the blow of never seeing him again, but things were different. I was different. It was just coffee.

On Thanksgiving eve, I usually did all the baking, the stuffing for the turkey, and a few special sides to bring to dinner. I was coming out of the worst time of my life, and my parents told me to just come and enjoy. I obeyed and used the quiet time alone to move forward in my life.

"Lord, I first repent for all of the wrong in this relationship—for losing my identity, for putting you last, and for losing my confidence in your promises. I release Juliàn today. I forgive him, and I repent for anything I did or said that displeased you. I thank you for your grace in every situation. I release him and his family. I vow to you that I am done. I will not go back. Right now, as your daughter, I make a demand on my covenant with you. I will NOT wait a year or two or three for my husband! I believe you have him for me, and I want a quick work. I trust you as I move forward. I believe my bread is coming home. I pray this believing you are faithful, in the name of Jesus."

I prayed that prayer with fervor and I know He always hears me. My situation turned around that night. I was sure. I released him and forgave him and myself while moving ahead. I knew that when I put a demand on the God I trusted, He would come through, just like He did when I was twelve years old, and hundreds of times since then.

Thanksgiving this year was a time of cleansing—renewal, a milestone, a new start. I had followed Lorenzo's advice and was spending more and more time with him and his wife. In fact, I was going to his house daily, meeting new people and really enjoying fellowship.

I had learned about some well-known singers from Brazil. They were top-notch, and I could find them on the Internet to fill in between the times when I couldn't hear Gabby and Lorenzo sing live to me.

When I arrived at my father's on Thanksgiving morning, I felt different. Open. Clean. Light. I cannot really explain it other than that. The oppression had broken. Though it felt strange not to be busy scampering around the kitchen with the family as usual, it felt so free. I went to one of the rooms where a computer was and started looking at Brazilian worship songs in Portuguese on YouTube. As I listened to familiar tunes and different lyrics, tears of gratefulness escaped my eyes, in thanks to God for anything and everything good.

My dad walked in with the "mappine" over his shoulder (the towel that was always there when he cooked, affectionately called that in Italian).

"What are you watching, honey?" my father asked as he looked at the screen.

After I explained who it was and what it was and he commented on how great it was, he called Lorenzo to laugh about the fact that I was watching worship in Portuguese. I knew there was a greater significance.

I cannot put into words how I felt that day. The weight of the world was finally off my shoulders. Tears flowed freely down my face in a cleansing, healing stream. It still amazes me how God will always meet you wherever you are—no matter how far, however wrong. The wrong road never becomes the right road, no matter how far you go on it. At some point, you must go back to where you first got off. Once you do, you reset your course and God is there to not bring you back but move you forward. Never let your history determine your destiny.

And just like that, my destiny had been set back on track.

Chapter 38

For Me to Go Under, God Would Have to Fail

Marriage is not always ordained by God. Religious people have this strange belief that if you are married, you have to stay married "no matter what." What a ridiculous concept—stay punished for the rest of your life because you made a mistake, a poor choice, or whatever may be. Marriage and relationships are complicated, gray areas. They are areas we, who are not actually part of the marriage and family dynamic, have no business judging. Most issues rarely fit neatly in black-and-white boxes. God's amazing grace has already forgiven our sins and our future mistakes before they are even committed. We can choose to end a marriage in divorce, knowing it is actually God's will for our life. Really? *Really.* The idea that everyone who is married should stay married is ridiculous. We judge with little consideration of how and when the marriage began and how the relationship ensued. We do not consider the circumstances surrounding the union and during it. I think this is primitive and judgmental. I think this is a punishing law, and I think this mentality often prevents God's will from freely flowing in our lives. It stops us from being with the right one, the one we can not only be happy with but the one who will help us fulfill our greatest potential in life. There are people stuck in marriages that are holding them back from being and doing everything they were created to be and do because "important" people have advised them to "work it out" or "stay together for the kids," or that "divorce is not an option." I think we need to see people and situations not only for what they are but for what they are not. This is not to say one should ever take marriage lightly with the option of divorce in one's mind. It is a sacred contract that should be done with prayerful consideration and time and the highest hopes.

There is an evil force that works against us. It is not nearly as powerful as the light that works on our behalf, but is consistently working to stop the good in our lives and distract us from our focus. Its purpose is to rob us of everything good promised and to destroy. The good news is that when we follow the light and resist the temptation to surrender to every single thing that tries to block, stop, and deflect it, the path gets brighter. We just have to walk and trust and believe in this good God.

Bad decisions do not define us, and they cannot trap us unless we allow them too. We have to move forward. We should not walk through life with regret, but we should remember the things in our lives we have come through and draw from the wisdom they provide. Mindful of the mistakes and poor choices, we must move forward, careful to learn from them and change, lest we repeat them. We must also be thankful that we have the opportunity to begin again.

*****

It was Monday afternoon, and I had just arrived again at Lorenzo's for daily "music therapy" and anything else they had to do that would distract me from remembering what I did not have. I rang the bell to let them know I was there and then let myself in. They were so good at helping to build me up. This had become a custom. It was Monday. I had been sitting at the dining room table in comfy clothes that were (finally) a step up from sweat clothes. My hair was curly. I usually like to blow it out straight, but I had opted for soft, long curls that day—not a look I felt good in, but I wasn't looking to impress anyone either. My dark hair contrasted with my pale, winter skin, and I still was not using makeup like I should have been; but at least my hair wasn't in a ponytail, and I wasn't wearing all black. I was settling in at the table, sipping on iced water, when the doorbell rang. It was just after 5:00 p.m. Gabby opened the door, and PJ walked in dressed in a suit with a backpack over one shoulder.

"You know PJ, right, Cyn?" Lorenzo asked.

PJ reminded his friend that we met and how heavy the couches were that they had moved at my house that summer. He chuckled and rolled his eyes, probably thinking about how heavy the couches were. I could not look in his eyes. He seemed so gentle. I knew nothing about him except what Lorenzo told me. I learned that he was Brazilian too and that they played soccer with a bunch of other Brazilian guys on Monday nights. He had even begun to play professionally in Brazil at one point as a preteen. (This American girl thought that was so cool.)

PJ was everything on my "list" and a whole lot more. He was committed to God, young and strong, olive skinned, gentle, ethnic, multilingual, soft-spoken. He was obviously athletic and broad shouldered and a pretty good drummer as well. *STOP, CYNTHIA! Focus—you have to get over your "stuff."*

Gabby offered PJ something, and he sat sort of across from me at the table. He just looked at my pale white, makeupless face without expression and gently said, *"I really like your hair like that. It looks nice."*

As I mentioned, my hair was big and really curly and dark, and it was my least favorite way to wear it. I reacted to his compliment in a way I have since learned not too. I rolled my eyes, touched my hair, and said, *"Yuck. I hate it like this."*

"Really? I like it. I think it looks really pretty," he said, ever so sweetly, staring at my eyes. He was staring at me, sitting closer now, to the right of me at the table. His expression never changed. I wished I could read his thoughts because he was lost in them. It made me shift in my seat and call out to Lorenzo to break the moment. Thankfully, Lorenzo came right away.

We ate, and PJ went to change into soccer clothes. Lorenzo asked us to go and watch them play. I was about to refuse, feeling my usual insecurities. Right about then, PJ came from the bathroom and said (like he had been practicing), *"Hey, ummmm, why don't you and Gabby come watch us play soccer tonight?"*

Lorenzo had been busting my chops every Monday since I started my "therapy" at his house, and I really did not want to go. The usual reasons to not participate in something social started floating in my head, and the anxiety I often dealt with to do something new was trying hard to edge out the desire to go. But since I was not ready to go home, I obliged them. I did feel a bit out of place at first, but I was excited inside.

When we arrived, I felt anxious. Between Lorenzo's protective, brotherly stance and PJ's soft sweet way and kind eyes, I felt safe. I remember feeling so proud of this handsome and athletic soccer man walking in front of me, slowly, so I could be close. I felt safe and special and protected walking behind him. His stride was confident and strong, but sweet. I never let him know, but it was secret bliss. I could not remember the last time I felt that way, but I knew it had been a long, long time ago. Way before Juliàn, if I had ever felt that way near him at all.

The night was great. It was so exciting to see them play. I felt young, alive, like I was in high school. GET A GRIP, CYN. I had to stop fantasizing. I was older, very imperfect, and preparing myself not to be disappointed even if I was interested. We went back to Gabby and Lorenzo's for pizza and soda, laughing and eating and drinking, and I didn't want the night to end. When reality set in and we had to go, I tried to quiet my excitement. I told myself PJ was just a nice guy and there was no way he could be into me. Besides, I needed time to get over Juliàn…didn't I?

Chapter 39

Perfect

I t is not news that we live in a sensational, superficial world that puts a higher value on a body than on a heart. For many years, I struggled with the fact that I was not born with a perfect body. Ha! Perfect is pretty funny because actually, I am way on the other end of that word. Anyone who knew anything about life and how I always thought poorly of myself, would say my struggle to lose the protective extra layer(s) of fat on my body had something to do with the "ick" of my childhood. I spent many years literally starving myself and working out in the gym until I could not move. Seriously. I have spent so many hours in the gym for so many years, and yet I never seemed to get where I wanted to be. I dreamt about being perfect and more. I dreamt I could meet the perfect man of my dreams and he would love me just like I was—far less than perfect. I wanted to be thin for this, but really what I needed was acceptance, pure and kind.

*****

Decide That You Want It More Than You Are Afraid of It

Lorenzo had been talking to PJ and me a lot separately, although neither of us knew this at the time. We had both been spending most of our free time at his house, and it was always a lot of fun. PJ was a musician—an amazing self-taught drummer who had been playing since he was very young. He also became part of my "music therapy." (It really was not just for me, but I pretended it was.) They were working on music to play together with the worship team. I secretly recorded them on my iPhone and replayed my favorites.

PJ began to talk to me about his life. What I did not know was that he had gone through a bad breakup too, much worse than mine. He was married at a young age, and from what I understood, it became unhappy very fast. He very softly described some of the things that transpired, and he explained how he was not "wired" for divorce. He came from a very happy, functional family. The disappointment and his desire to fix what was wrong and make everything right nearly broke him. When we could talk alone, he would speak about the pain of his relationship and how he could not believe he was in this position. He further explained that he had a son who was born thirteen months after he was married and was the subject of a prophecy he had received about a year before. He described the deep pain of not being able to live with him as a happy family and how terribly he missed Jordon during the week. He said it was the hardest thing in the world to leave him and to lose the marriage and family he had dreamt of his whole life, but that he had no choice because her heart just was not in it at all.

For a fleeting moment, as I listened to PJ talk about leaving his house and his son, I felt a flutter of hope and imagined that Juliàn too could leave his baby and see her on the weekends, to be with me. I quickly caught myself and let go of that thought to prevent me from falling back into a trap. I thought about how we sometimes become so fixated, so enveloped in our own pain. In that moment, I felt such compassion for PJ. I felt that what he endured was far worse than what I did, and I realized how quickly my healing was manifesting. My sight was returning. My eyes were opening, the blinders had fallen off.

Although PJ was easy to talk to, and I loved his gentleness, I had already told Lorenzo not to even think about telling us to be together. I was quite sure I had no romantic interest in him even though he was so handsome, and when he spoke, I just wanted to stay and listen and let his soft, strong voice wash over me because I just felt safe. He spoke with a gentleness and with a kindness I had not felt from a man, other than my father, in a very long time. More than my thought that I was not interested in him, I knew he would not be interested in me. He had described his ex-wife as "beautiful" more than once, and she knew his first language. They had a child together, and though they hadn't been together for more than a year, she was legally still his wife. I was older than him, very American, very imperfect, and preparing myself not to be disappointed, even if I was a little bit interested.

It was quite remarkable how similar PJ and Juliàn were at a glance—both so handsome, athletic, and exotic. They were both born in another country, and both grew up speaking another language. They both experienced emigration to this great United States of America. They had similar coloring, and both were gentle and soft-spoken. If you glanced quickly and did not know them, you might confuse them. But the light in PJ's eye was more than just the twinkle in Juliàn's. Major differences in character (and the lack thereof) differentiated the two immensely. As I began to spend time getting to know PJ, learning who he was and where he came from, I wanted to know more. He had an almost intimidating, strong sense of family, values, and commitment. He was dedicated to God and church work, and he made no apologies for this. His free time was spent playing soccer or playing drums at church. His values were so transparent. It was clear that he honored God and his family with his whole heart. He was good to his parents, and had always respected and supported them. PJ was also a soccer player, and he too had the chance to play professional soccer in Brazil. He often talked about his passion for the "greatest sport in the world." He explained that his father coached professional soccer players in Brazil and had real knowledge of both the game and what it took to be great at playing it. PJ was good enough to play professionally as a young teenager. In Brazil, this is not uncommon, but his dream to play on that level could not be realized when he and his family moved to America. He was a strong athlete with big defined caramel-colored arms. His masculine legs were thick and strong with noticeable definition. PJ was a self-taught drummer who began playing in churches in Brazil as a child and eventually played in concerts and stadiums as a teenager because he worked hard at being that good. A committed Christian, and the son of loving parents, he was also father to a young son whom he would do anything for, and he actually did. PJ spoke with such a gentleness, and he listened so intently when I spoke. He was just tall enough, handsome, and his oh-so-lovely light-brown eyes looked oh-so-kind.

This man was so different than what I had known, and I wanted to know more. I wanted to know more and more about him and his son. I wanted to hear more about Brazil. I wanted to hear him and Lorenzo laugh and talk and argue and pray in Portuguese. So I decided we could just have fun and be friends, and we did, and we were.

As we continued to spend more and more time together, PJ kept softly insisting that I meet his son, Jordon, but I was petrified. I heard that Jordon's mother was pretty and thin. I had heard PJ talk about his son, and I knew that children were terribly honest. I had experienced that innocent honesty more times than I would like to admit with kids telling me I was fat or asking if I was pregnant. Ughhh. It is humiliating, and I had the feeling Jordon might do something like this because I knew from Lorenzo and Gabby that he was smart and outspoken and honest. The thing you fear the most can really come upon you, and oh, how I feared kids. I kept insisting that it was not time yet, and PJ kept respecting my feelings.

Lorenzo was really good at being the catalyst to elicit a reaction. One Sunday during church, he invited me to come over for lunch. I knew PJ was spending the weekend with his son, so I let it be and spoke to him on the phone. Lorenzo could not leave well enough alone. While I sat on his couch watching TV with Gabby after eating a nice lunch, he secretly called PJ and invited him to come over with Jordon to join us.

Hearing the doorbell ring with virtually no time to prepare to cover my body and hide from five-and-a-half-year-old Jordon, I grabbed the nearest blanket and covered everything but my toes, which were painted a pretty hot pink and looking okay. Jordon marched through the door with a huge grin on his face, saying hello to everyone, and came right over.

"Hi, I'm Jordon, who are you? What's wrong with your feet?" he asked, noticing my second toes were longer than my big toes and probably noticing the small red bumps on the same toes and on the fourth ones as well. PJ was right behind him, chuckling and shaking his head while turning a light shade of red. To my delight, he didn't really realize Jordon's question. As horrified as I was about the "feet" comment, he didn't mention my body at all and I breathed a temporary sigh of relief, thinking that would probably come later.

PJ said hello, kissed my cheek, and sat down next to me as he asked how I was. Jordon had already raced to get his backpack so he could bust it open to show me his homework assignment.

"Do you want to help me do my homework?" he asked expecting that I would say yes, with enthusiasm and the cutest voice with a tiny lisp.

I could see Lorenzo grinning widely and gesturing for me to go help. Never missing any opportunity to say what he thought, he mused, *"You know, PJ will be testing you to see if you will be a good mother."* If I could have slapped him, I would have. I glared at Lorenzo and happily walked to the dining room table to help Jordon with, of all things, human anatomy.

This was the beginning of a beautiful ride with Jordon. He is full of life and just as handsome as his beautiful father. He is a kind and gentle soul, a sort of carbon copy of his father in every way yet with his own unique edge. He is my sweet friend. I have this amazing opportunity to pour into him and help him become the man God made him to be. He is another unbelievable gift from God to me—"two for the price of one." Only God can do that.

Chapter 40

Change

I feel like I am in a new place, but I am still me. I know that I have access to and abide in grace to do what I need to, but I am still me. I believe in the power I have received! It is just that I am still walking in the same body and thinking with the same mind even though my thoughts are different. Ha! I sound crazy. But I'm not. I face this day with a renewed and resolved will and spirit, but I look like I did yesterday; and sometimes, the key fits the lock, but it doesn't turn. Will it turn? Yes…YES! Of course it will fit and turn! Not turning represents the past, not today; but today, it is okay. Today, the key fits. It turns, it unlocks, it opens. Now, I have to walk through.

I spoke to a young girl today. She is in her early twenties. I've spoken to her before. She is sweet, cute, and so friendly. She's a dialysis technician. She learned to do what she does after a six-month training period, shadowing a preceptor and then passing some exams. She is a high point in my day when I go to a clinic and see her working. She is kind to patients, always with a bright, bubbly smile and a kind word or a sweet funny gesture. She is respectful and observant and always apt to help. When I first met her, I tried to guess her ethnicity. She heard me talking to a nurse about his native country, Guyana, and she asked me if I spoke Portuguese when she heard me say my husband was Brazilian. She told me she was a mix of nations and cultures and could speak Spanish, a little Portuguese, and another language that I cannot remember. After that day, whenever I would see her, we would start talking about careers, and I encouraged her to continue her education, become a registered nurse, and maybe eventually a nurse practitioner or a physician assistant, like me. We would talk about my career and her dreams, usually with whomever else was there with us. I have seen her several more times since we first met, and we seem to always continue our conversations where we last left off. We talk about patients and work and then we cover a lot of subjects, like pop culture, men, music, and even food and culture.

I saw her again today, and I realized it had been quite a while since I had seen her last. Our conversation went the same way as it had previously. She asked a few questions about my career path and experience, and I answered her, offering ideas and suggestions to her. I had a bit more time today, so I probed deeper about her life and interests, encouraging her to pursue her dreams. For some reason, I had assumed she was living home and everything was perfect and normal.

She told me today that she has a two-year-old daughter whom she lives alone with. I continued to probe and came to find out that the father of her daughter is in prison and gives her and her daughter zero support. He never did. She hesitantly continued with her cute smile and little laughs, explaining that it was "all fine," that they were both better off without him. I asked her if she gets help from her mother and father. She went on to explain that her father was never really around and that her mom died of cancer a few weeks ago. She had battled her cancer for a year, but it had aggressively metastasized and robbed her life. Almost speechless, and moved with compassion, I smiled easily at her still-jovial expression. Not once in that time did I hear a negative word or regret. Not once did I hear it was difficult or impossible or that she felt tired or stressed. Not once did she frown or shudder or say, "Life sucks" or "It has been so bad." In that moment, I felt so small and so wrong for making my pain and my difficulties so big when really, they were nothing compared to many other people's realities.

There is always going to be someone with a sadder story or a harder situation to overcome. Our approach to what life throws our way, and the attitude with which we handle even the hardest things will determine the outcome. No matter how hard or easy things are, how we face it, regardless of how it feels will determine the impact it has on us.

We must decide how we will approach life. In fact, we must decide every day to get up and dream and focus and prepare to fulfill the dreams. It all starts in our mental approach—in our thinking— and it trickles down to our words and how we live out what we want.

*****

Soccer

Mondays started to become my favorite day of the week. I lived for Mondays—*Segunda-feira*, as my new Brazilian friends called it. I was spending almost every day with Lorenzo and Gabby, but Mondays were special. I would go there right after work, and PJ would come a few minutes after me. Monday was his early night at work—his only early night, and I secretly looked forward to seeing him and learning more and more about him. I started caring about what I was going to wear and thinking about how I was doing my hair in the morning. I started sleeping better at night, and it became easier to get out of bed in the morning.

By six o'clock on Monday nights, we would decide what was for dinner. Until dinner arrived or we finished making it, my music therapy sessions would take place. After we ate and cleaned up, it was time to get ready for soccer, which started at nine. Soccer was a sport I told people for many years was boring, hard to follow, and that I had no interest in. PJ and Lorenzo had already changed my mind. I loved watching them play their hearts out on that indoor field in the sports complex. I loved videoing them on my iPhone and show-ing them later. Although I was really shy to be there and always felt embarrassed, I liked meeting up with a lot of the guys they played with. They made me feel welcome and normal. I met PJ's kind and funny brother and his warm and fun loving cousins and slowly began to discover the wide world of Brazilian and world-class soccer and just how much those Brasileiros love it.

On the nights I chose not to go and watch soccer, I would stay with Gabby. Many times, we would sit on the couch, searching the Internet comparing what we wanted to buy or attempt to watch a movie on TV. I would usually end up napping on the couch next to her. It was almost like I was catching up on my rest—not necessarily sleep, but true rest. She was always encouraging me softly with a hint of a Brazilian accent, *"Relax, Cintchya," "Make yourself comfortable, Cintch,"* and then a sweet little giggle—a little like Betty Rubble from the Flintstones. She was always forcing tea or coffee on me in a cute cup and saucer of fine china. Those little details made the tea a bit sweeter and the moment a bit more special. I loved resting there on that couch, which is pretty ironic because it was the one I gave to them because I hated it so much when it was mine. I felt so warm and safe there, waiting for Lorenzo and PJ, who would be back soon. I thought about how much I enjoyed the comfort of resting in their home on the couch I had given them on the first day I met PJ. Maybe that was partly what made resting on the couch so special. It was symbolic of our first meeting. Being there on that velvety brown couch in that apartment that was always warmer than what I usually liked, was just a special time of my life. It was dark and warm and almost spa-like, and it actually felt like love was free-flowing and so very tangible. I remember the feelings that came over me waiting for PJ and Lorenzo while we sipped and chatted about whatever came to our minds. I felt happy. I felt safe. I just felt good.

When the boys would come storming through the door at around ten forty-five, flapping away in Portuguese, full of energy and hungry for something, it was so exciting for me. Although the calm atmosphere would change, it was still so warm and pleasant. If I was tired and had to get home, I loved when Lorenzo would insist we stay and talk and eat and throw caution to the wind about waking up for work the next day. We would oblige him and have a snack and talk until we could not talk any longer. We would say our good-byes, and PJ and I would walk out together, headed to our cars. He never seemed to make it to his car. He would walk me to mine and sit in it and we would talk for hours, and when we would realize the time, maybe around 2:00 or 3:00 a.m., we would force ourselves to say good night and drive to our homes, talking on the phone the entire time. We would say good-bye, and I would rush to brush my teeth and wash my face and would jump into bed, waiting for him to text. Most times we would text until 4:00 or 5:00 a.m. or until one of us could not stay awake. In times like those, sleep is secondary. All the energy you have goes into getting to know someone. For some reason, there was just so much to talk about.

One freezing cold December night, after so many Mondays-night good-byes with friendly hugs and kisses on my cheeks, PJ leaned over to kiss me good-night. He was so brave and gentle and kind, placing his hands on my face to warm it up. I felt like a school-girl. I didn't want it to ever end. I remember thinking about all the things that had transpired so recently in my life. I recounted the promises I believed in so strongly and smiled because the worst really was over. In the wee hours of the morning, when I could barely think and everything was quiet enough that I could float in and out of a dreamlike trance, I would remember how I had hoped and believed and visualized what my husband would be like. I remembered the stranger who sent my dad a message that sounded so insane if you did not understand the beauty of the Bible and the irony of the statement, and I realized what she prophesied, without knowing anything had now been realized—my bread was finally home.

Chapter 41

Bread

Today I am just grateful. There is nothing special happening that I can speak of. In fact, there are challenges to overcome. I am tired and feeling a little weak, but inside, I am strong. I am recovering from an infectious bug, and it is Monday. I have to work. I am waiting to pay off some things and feeling the pressure, but I see them paid. I am grateful. Most of what I have looked for in life thus far, I have. The things I do not have are just around the corner. I know this. I feel my heart softening more as I sense God's presence increase in my life, and I am getting smaller. That doesn't mean I am not a strong, significant person in the world—not at all. It means as significant as I have become, it's all because of Him, through Him, and for Him, and I recognize it. I am not exactly the proudest person either. Me, proud? That's funny. Sometimes it is how I am perceived, but that really is funny because the truth is I question everything I do all the time. I used to apologize a lot, but not anymore. I am getting better and better at accepting and liking me. Humility is easy for me. My flaws used to be so big and visible, and some still are, but I am learning to rest in Him. I am kind of like a Ferrari. I cannot move without the driver or the fuel, but people only notice the car. In reality, it is just metal, rubber, leather, and glass that is simply nice to look at, but pretty useless without the driver. God is the driver. Someone once said God was their copilot. Not for me. He is definitely the pilot. I am letting Him chart the course, and I am following orders. My heart is full today. I cannot think of much or do anything without welling up with tears. I used to fight this softness, but I cannot fight it anymore. I am a beautiful, valuable, exotic car going on an amazing ride, full speed ahead, with the driver of all drivers taking the wheel.

*****

Painted pink toes buried in the cool white sand of a breezy, warm Caribbean beach. Sipping an icy tropical drink from a freshly-scooped-out coconut cold enough to quench my thirst and balanced enough to satisfy my sweet tooth. Giant, beautiful, fluffy snowflakes gently dancing down on my face and tongue, and the air is refreshingly cool but not freezing. Wearing any clothes I want and looking and feeling beautiful no matter what size I am. This is life with PJ. He is beautiful on the inside and out, but that is just the beginning. His kindness is noticed by everyone almost immediately, and he is respectful and sensitive to them. He is so soft inside, but oh so strong! His love is easy. He learned this love from two of the most loving people I have come to know—his parents. They live a life with purpose and respect for God, each other, and their family. There is purity of heart. There is conviction. There is laughter. There is an innocence that cannot be mistaken. I deserve this. The darkness of the past fades every day as I step deeper into this relationship, and I feel safe. I feel protected. Sometimes I fight this great thing that has happened. I take my feelings of insecurity, wrap them in a ball, and throw it at him with vigor. He catches it and handles it. My toes are back in the sand.

*****

My father really liked PJ. He constantly told me this. I invited him and my stepmother over for dinner. They accepted my invitation for dinner at my house to get to know him. When they sat down and began chatting with us, PJ was gentle and respectful, listening much more than he talked. After just a few minutes of this, PJ stood up and decided he would officially tell my parents his intentions. I felt flushed and shy since I had no idea he would do that. My heart melted as I watched him bravely win my father's heart, declaring his plan for our lives together.

"I just want you to know, I have every intention of honoring you and your daughter. I will never hurt her or you. I want to be with her, and I want your blessing."

I have said so many times how much he is like my dad and that it is remarkable how the God I trust and continue to trust more deeply every day could bring me this loving person from a culture five thousand miles away. Yet it truly is as if he is my own father's son, raised by his own father who is amazing in his own right. The love comes in many ways. Sometimes it is correcting. Sometimes it is caressing. Sometimes it is soft. Sometimes is it hard. It is constant. It is forward thinking and forgiving.

My parents thanked him for his honesty and boldness. Their faces were glowing as we laughed, listening to my dad's jokes from the old Italian church. We all enjoyed my feast of deliciously golden-brown fried chicken cutlets; buttery mashed potatoes; asparagus oreganato with fresh herbs, grated cheese, and lemon; fresh broccoli sautéed in garlic and oil; and a mixed green salad with beets, walnuts, and goat cheese.

After that great night with my parents and PJ's sweet expression of his motives, we had a lot of trouble staying away from each other. We decided that was not even an option. Over the next few months as we laughed and loved and learned, we talked marriage and, with both of our parents' blessings, set a wedding date.

Chapter 42

Grace

*G*race is a word we take a little bit too lightly. We sing "Amazing Grace" as ritual in church on Sundays, dressed in our best, and smiling through the reality of our lives. Somehow, we do not really grasp that the writer of this poem, John Newton, realized and lived the power of that grace. He recognized that this grace that came to us from a good God, who left heaven to take upon him the form of a servant and became a man. He humbled himself in obedience to feel what we feel and suffer what we suffer. This is the thing that makes Christianity so different than all the world religions. A majestic God, the Creator of all, sent his Son, who humbled Himself as a man to feel what we feel and to take our place. The grace, now exalted, ever lives for us. Jesus is grace, and accepting him welcomes a life of love and abundance. We do not earn it. We do not deserve it, and yet we are never ever denied it. We just have to believe it. We just have to receive it. It is a free gift. The interesting thing that is inexplicable is that Jesus becomes for us whatever it is we need. If we need healing, we receive healing. If it is confidence we need to pursue, we receive confidence. If it is for a relationship, we believe and receive that he becomes the key to heal or fix it, and He does. This is an amazing, indescribable, overwhelming gift. We just have to breathe in and accept with expectation for the need to be met and our lives to be changed. There are days when it is easy to accept and receive. There are even some days when though we accept and believe, we do not see or feel a difference immediately. In the actual process of believing and receiving, this amazing grace will work out some of the other major issues in our lives. Issues like learning patience and developing a strategy to overcome the mountains we face. The grace is Jesus, and He is the answer and all that you need even when you are not fully convinced.

*****

When we decided we would be married, not too many months after meeting, PJ and I were spending a lot of time together, talking. We discussed everything we could think of, learning more and more about each other, our lives, our cultures and families, and our faith in God. I am a strong person with a drive to succeed and accomplish, but I am soft in relationships. I am truly a lover and not a fighter, so I was trying to live this way and avoid conflict at all costs, which is in sharp contrast to all the conflict in my past. I had experienced the goodness of God, as did PJ. I had been developing an understanding of God's unmerited favor and kindness and an understanding of the fact that I could not earn my relationship with God at all. This concept is frowned upon in religion. Many are taught that we must earn our relationship and that good acts made us closer to God. This is humanity at its worst and best. The human condition to do good is a godly concept, but it does not make God love us more.

PJ and I were taking a ride south, away from Newark, where we had just finished eating at one of the Brazilian steakhouses (Churrasquerias). We feasted at a delicious Brazilian buffet of well-known appetizers and specialties like rice and black beans, mayonnaise, salpicão (shredded chicken salad with the addition of raisins and carrots and potato sticks), fresh beets and other vegetables and salads, fried mandioca (yucca), farofa, fried bananas—even lasagna and various stews—and so much more. That all came before the actual grilled meat fest of both beef and pork ribs, chicken and linguiça (sausages), and almost every cut of beef you could imagine, and of course the glorious picanha (pee-ki-nya)—the best cut of top sirloin bathed in salt and grilled to perfection on a giant skewer then sliced tableside.

Feeling satiated and happy with my hand in his as he drove my car over the Driscoll bridge, he began to talk about something with a very heavy judgmental slant that sounded nothing like the PJ I was getting to know so well. He was recounting a lot of the jargon learned in church about judging people rather than praying for them, and when I started to express that I disagreed completely, his hand let go of mine, and tension began to rise. He became adamant about this "fact" learned in church that really had no grasp on the profound love of a Heavenly Father. I knew that PJ had begun to believe and experience this great goodness of God in a way that obliterated the religious mind-set, but he was fighting it as he was learning. I remember thinking if he cannot let go of this thinking, we will hit a wall. PJ raised his voice and told me that there was a standard, and although I believe that, it has never been the job of the church to judge, only to love and let God judge, and I remember seeing his angry face all the way home. The more we discussed the unconditional love and grace of God for *everyone*, the angrier and louder he became. Conflict about the very subject we loved the most. We arrived home, and I remember thinking, *Lord let him get it, because if he doesn't get it, I am going to have to be out of here.* (I may have even said it to PJ.)

It took some reading and talking and thinking and more talking over the next few weeks, and PJ began to let go of some of the ideals he had worked so hard to develop. I saw that kind heart of his begin to grasp this grace for every day. The warmth of PJ's love toward me and his son and family, which truly was the love of our God toward me, began to replace the mentality of the church as he saw it. *This* was the grace for life that could rewrite anyone's story. God never sent Jesus to the world to condemn it. He sent Him to love us and to be saved from our own thinking, saved from our own mistakes, saved from whatever evil tried to overtake us.

Chapter 43

Light

Light! Glorious beams of warmth, radiance, brightness, and beauty. Sun and all that it seems to represent as clear, beautiful, and welcoming. The sun is shining brightly, not literally outside but all around me. I feel it on my face and—mmm—it is so delicious.

I love the color of my bedroom. A warm grayish-purply blue so inviting that it makes you want to jump into it and bathe in it. I look up. It is on the ceiling too, just a shade darker, not too much, just enough. This color is in the center on the highest part of the ceiling, the tray, and it looks so pretty. It is the end of a long day. Nighttime has come, the last act in the play of another day of work and life and all the things that pull you in twenty-nine directions. For some reason, although it is night, there is so much light tonight. Light that is bright white and happy, yellow and warm. It is streaming, glistening sunlight in my room. Outside, the wind is blowing so hard, and it is cold and windy and icy rainy—but I am in paradise. The sun is beaming down on my bare skin, and I am sipping an icy cold drink with a little umbrella sticking out of it. The beam embraces me. I am so content that it is making me feel a bit ashamed. More people should feel this way. *It is not really fair to have all you ever dreamed of,* I think as I drift into sleep, his breath on my neck. His hands—I love his hands—are touching me so sweetly, moving less and less until we both are asleep.

I wake up and look at my husband quietly lying there beside me. Husband. I say it again in my mind. H-U-S-B-A-N-D. His beautiful profile and strong body warms my heart and the whole room. It has been eight months, and it still feels so strange to say it, *"my husband."* He loves me, and ohhhh, so much! So much more than I deserve. So much more than I ever believed possible. Whenever I stumble into thinking he does not, he is quicker than a speeding bullet to reassure me. He senses my insecurity like a talented, old sleuth and soothes my doubts. My wonderful father takes pleasure in telling me how much my husband loves me. He sees it so clearly, much more clearly than I do, though the feelings are undeniable. It is abundant. Life is so good.

*****

As PJ and I talked about and prepared for our future together, I could not believe it. I was actually preparing for my wedding. We can be so foolish sometimes, can't we? We hope and believe and plan for our dream, it happens, and then we cannot believe it! I had this amazing guy who was deep and intelligent. He was forward-thinking, yet traditional about all the right things like loving one woman and caring for his family and being hard-working as well as being as sexy and handsome as they come. He wanted *me*. He did not want me to change and become perfect to be with him. He wanted me. He was planning to marry me. He was the one for me. The celebration of this love had already begun and we would officially celebrate with our friends and family on October 20.

Epilogue

This is the just the beginning of my story. There is a lot more to come.

What I have learned so far is that you do not have to wait to be perfect to be loved or to enjoy where you are in life. We grow up reading about princesses and models and super athletes that seem to be perfect people with perfect lives. They are all just stories. Real people have real ups and downs. They face obstacles and pursue their passions. It is never too late to pursue your passions. I thought that for a long time. I was sure I could only meet a handsome, intelligent, athletic, kind, man who complemented me if I was near-perfect-bodied, twenty-three years old, and had some kind of world-class something. I was sure I could never see my destiny fulfilled if I was not at least average-body-sized, let alone skinny! Lord, if I passed age thirty with no husband and no children, I should just quit already. Thank God I was so wrong. This does not mean I am totally content either. I want to be better in every way possible—physically, mentally, and spiritually. Life truly is a journey. A potpourri of knowledge and experiences coming together to make a unique imprint in the world for some purpose.

For years, I secretly punished myself for so many of my wrongs but never rewarded myself for my *rights*. I couldn't even see any of my rights! There were always good people trying to show me them, but I couldn't and wouldn't see until now. Healing comes in a lot of forms, but first, we have to forgive. We have to forgive ourselves and then everyone else even when they don't deserve it. Forgiveness is actually easy, and it releases you from the negative impact of a situation. When you choose to just let go of the anger and the pain and stop looking back, you will glide forward. For many of us, we are far from the ones who have hurt us, and forgiveness is even easier when you are physically far away.

Life is ultimately about our destiny. We have all had bad breaks—things we wished were different, things we wished we did differently. If God knew those things could stop you from your destiny, He never would have allowed it! Think about that, just for a moment or two. We were all made to succeed. We were all given the opportunity to realize what our ultimate destiny is even when it isn't all that clear through life's ups and downs. We were even given the strength to go for it no matter who or what tries to stop us.

We are loved unconditionally by a good God. We have the right to be loved by good people as well. Accepting this love makes life better because it changes our attitude, and this positions us to succeed. We must attempt, no matter how many times we have failed, to do whatever it is we feel called to accomplish. Failing does not make one a failure. Every morning brings new grace and new strength to move forward. Make good choices. Choose to believe you too are marked. Too many people say, "I'm scarred for life," referencing a traumatic experience or painful past. No! Those scars are covered with a divine mark from God. He did not scar you. He saved you and He marked you with His love and grace to overcome. His mark can push you toward your best life and erase the scars. His mark is all that matters.

I choose to walk this path. I choose to face and overcome hardship. I choose to use faith to confront and immobilize fear. I choose to change what I do not want, to remove that which harms me, and to engage in that which enriches. I choose to give and be more gracious. I choose to forgive. I choose to thrive rather than just survive. This path will become so bright, so clear and visible as we walk it. It will get brighter and brighter just like the sun rising and making us see in the day. It will be so bright that the darkness, the sadness, the negative, and the fear have no chance at all. This all really is impossible, until it happens, because with God, ALL things are possible!

Be encouraged by the lyrics of a very famous song by a friend of mine who has touched millions of people and has been a vessel through whom healing could flow. The words are translated from Portuguese and will encourage you. If you find the song on the Internet and you let her sing it to you, you will never be the same.

If they try to kill your dreams,
Suffocating your heart,
If they throw you to the lion's den,
and feeling hurt, you lost your vision
Don't give up, don't stop believing,
The dreams of God will never die

Receive the healing,
Receive the anointing,
The anointing of boldness,
The anointing to conquer,
The anointing to grow and overcome

Don't give up, don't stop fighting,
Don't stop worshipping,
Lift up your eyes and see
God is restoring your dreams
and your vision

Receive the healing,
Receive the anointing,
The anointing of boldness,
The anointing to conquer,
The anointing to grow and overcome

—Ludmila Ferber
"Sonhos De Deus"

About the Author

C ynthia Demola-Oliveira is the daughter of, David T. Demola a well-known international pastor and teacher. She spent a lot of her life in a supportive role with him as a volunteer and staff member until becoming a practicing physician assistant. Working mostly in the field of nephrology in the New York metropolitan area, Cynthia's life has been earmarked by service. She learned from her father to touch the lives of people with good news in any possible way and has always had a true passion to pursue that path. She has authored a book chronicling her life story thus far and serves alongside of her husband, Paulo Oliveira Junior (PJ), Pastor of MARKED CHURCH in New Jersey. Cynthia and PJ travel internationally preaching in English, Portuguese and Spanish. They reside with their son Jordon and their toy poodle Bella.

CPSIA information can be obtained
at www.ICGtesting.com
Printed in the USA
BVHW081153150722
642152BV00007B/245